100 Ways with Chicken

Anne Ager

 Letts **Guides**

Charles Letts and Company Ltd
London Edinburgh München and New York

First published 1978
by Charles Letts and Company Limited
Diary House, Borough Road, London SE1 1DW

Design and illustrations by Perera
Cover photograph by Chris Thomson

ISBN 0 850 97241 8

Printed in Great Britain by
Letts Erskine Limited, Dalkeith

Contents

Introduction   4

Chicken for starters   12

Chicken for the oven   18

Chicken for the pot   24

Chicken for the frying pan   29

Chicken for the grill   35

Chicken for cold dishes   40

Foreign ways with chicken   47

Chicken miscellania: sauces,
   stuffings and butters   56

Index   64

Introduction

Chicken is one of our most versatile foods, and yet we are inclined to cook it by only a few conventional methods. Indeed, to many people cooked chicken is no more than a plump, roasted bird with bread sauce and stuffing, and though this can be a delicious dish they are certainly missing many other tasty meals by only eating it this way. In this book I have tried to show how many different and interesting ways there are of using chicken – giving as many as one hundred recipes, including those for accompanying sauces, stuffings and savoury butters.

The chicken is a descendant of the wild jungle fowl of eastern Asia. The earliest known reference made to a chicken was about 570BC, which affords this domestic bird quite an enviable history. It is interesting to note that the Romans considered the red and black plumed hens to be the best layers, the white ones being regarded as delicate and inferior. At that time chickens were kept in poultry yards, where the ground was strewn with sand and ashes. The walls were fitted with roosting poles and nest boxes, and incubation was well practised by the Romans. Earlier,

the ancient Egyptians actually used ovens for hatching eggs. The Romans were also adept at breeding plump birds – balls of moistened wheat were fed regularly to the hens.

Poultry production has seen many changes, and it has developed into a fine art. Chicken is the general culinary term for the domestic fowl bred both for egg production and for the table. It covers a wide range of birds, from the small 4 to 6 week old poussins to the elderly laying hens which never reach the table. Within this range are also the spring chicken, or broilers, up to 3 lb in weight, 3 to 5 lb roasting chickens, and the large capon. The capon is fattened up to produce a bird the size of a small turkey or goose. And it is often roasted in the style of the larger fowl.

Chicken can be bought in many different forms. Free range chickens are still very popular, but the introduction of deep frozen chicken has made shopping and storage much easier. Both fresh and frozen chickens can be bought either as whole birds or in portions. Your butcher will prepare chicken according to your needs, provided he is given advance warning, and all supermarkets sell chicken joints such as breasts and drumsticks, either packed singly or in packs containing two or more. Chill chicken is another type of prepared chicken which is widely available. Unlike frozen chicken, it is not stored at an extremely low temperature. The whole birds or portions are guaranteed fresh, but they are as perishable as any other raw fresh meat.

To get the best from chicken you need to know what to look for when buying, how to store the bird safely, how to prepare it and how to cook it successfully. It is a common complaint, particularly with reference to frozen chicken, that 'chicken no longer has the same flavour'. This is a rather unfair judgement, a hankering for things past, rather than a statement of fact. Chicken is what you make it! If frozen and battery bred chicken is thawed correctly and cooked in an appetizing way it is every bit as good as its traditionally bred counterpart, the free range bird. The onus of producing tasty chicken lies with the cook!

Choosing and buying chicken

In choosing and buying chicken, good quality is of the utmost importance. The first general point in judging quality is to remember that prepacked chicken, whether fresh or frozen, is normally marked with a date to indicate its freshness and lasting quality. Don't abuse this date marking. It is there to safeguard the consumer.

Fresh and chill chickens and portions should have creamy white skin free of any discoloured patches and their flesh should be fresh pink in colour. Choose whole chickens that are well rounded and plump. They keep a better flavour and shape when cooked.

Boiling fowls tend to have a deposit of yellow fat just beneath the skin. Choose fowls that do not have excessive fat.

Frozen chicken is very difficult to assess as you cannot judge the bird by smell. Avoid frozen birds that are very dark in colour or blotchy as this usually means that they are not in prime condition. Check any 'sell by' or 'eat by' dates on the wrappers.

Whether you buy fresh or frozen chicken is very much a matter of personal preference. Fresh or frozen give the same cooked result if prepared in the correct manner. Buy according to your needs, bearing in mind the method of cooking you have planned. A $3\frac{1}{2}$ lb chicken for roasting will serve four people generously and a $4\frac{1}{2}$ to 5 lb bird will serve six. Some frozen chickens are sold with their giblets and some are not. If you want the giblets for stock or gravy check they are included before you buy.

Half chickens are a good buy for two people, either for roasting or grilling.

Chicken portions are usually an economical buy, and they ease the job of calculating how much chicken to allow per person: one chicken quarter gives one very generous portion; one thigh, breast or large drumstick gives one average portion, as do two wings or small drumsticks. Portions are particularly suitable for quick roasting, grilling, frying and casseroling.

Boiling fowl are very reasonably priced and one boiling fowl can serve a family of four twice. The bird can be cooked with vegetables to add moisture and flavour. The meat is then usually removed from the bone to use in made-up dishes. Add half the boned cooked meat to a curry sauce, for example, and the other half to a white sauce with mushrooms. The liquid from a cooked boiling fowl makes an excellent base for sauces and soups.

Storing chicken

Chicken is a highly perishable commodity and needs sensible, careful storage.

Fresh uncooked chicken should be stored, either uncovered or lightly covered with foil, in the refrigerator preferably for no more than 24 hours. Always remove the butcher's wrapping as this can harbour bacteria and cause the chicken to sweat.

Likewise, **prepacked chill chicken** should either be removed from its original wrapper or the cellophane be broken so that the chicken can breathe.

Cooked chicken should be kept for no more than 24 hours in the refrigerator. To prevent it drying out, wrap it loosely in cling wrap or foil before storing. Remember that cooked chicken dries out more quickly if it is left on the bone.

It is best to thaw **deep frozen chicken** slowly before cooking. Leave the chicken in its freezer wrapping, but break the seal. Thaw in the refrigerator for the appropriate length of time. A $3\frac{1}{2}$ lb chicken will take approximately 14 hours and chicken joints 4 to 6 hours, depending on their size.

Ensure that ready frozen chicken which you intend to keep in a freezer for future use has not started to thaw before you store it.

Freezing chicken

Chicken you plan to freeze yourself must be very fresh. Remove the giblets as these are best frozen separately. Wrap the chicken, either whole or jointed, in freezer foil or wrap, making sure that the bones or sharp corners do not puncture the wrapping. Chicken can be frozen in this way for up to 12 months.

Trussing a whole chicken

Some chickens are sold ready trussed. This can make stuffing the bird rather difficult, so it is best to loosen the string beforehand and then retruss the chicken yourself. This is not a difficult procedure and it ensures that the chicken is

properly stuffed and retains a good shape when cooked – no spreadeagled wings or joints separating from the body!

There are several methods of trussing. Here is the simplest and most effective. Stuff the chicken before you start. Remove the end pieces from the feet if this has not been done already. Push a skewer through the fleshy part of the leg so that it goes right through the bird and through the leg on the opposite side. This holds the bird in shape ready for the next stage (see illustration A).

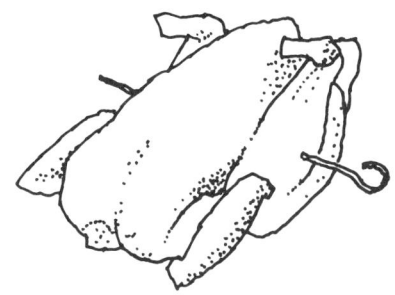

A

Turn the bird breast downwards and fold the neck flap over the back of the chicken. Insert a skewer into one wing, pushing it through the neck flap and then through the wing on the opposite side (see illustration B).

B

Turn the chicken the right way up.
Tie the ends of the legs neatly
together with string, enclosing the
parson's nose (see illustration C).

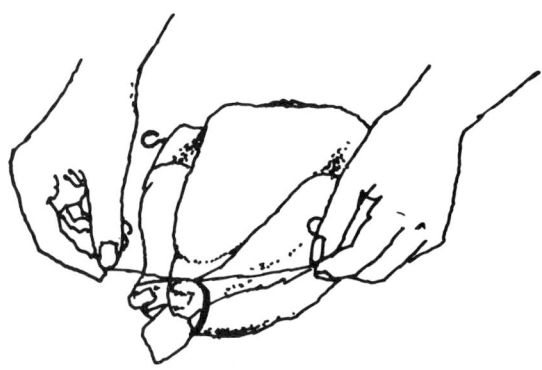

C

Cooking chicken

Chicken is suitable for most
methods of cooking, as the following recipe sections illustrate. The
most important thing to remember
is that chicken needs added moisture
whichever cooking method is used.
With roasting, grilling and frying,
fat is used, and frequent basting is
necessary in roasting and grilling to
keep the flesh succulent. With
boiling and casseroling it is liquid
that keeps the chicken moist.

Carving chicken

Carving by some people involves
pulling at each of the joints of the
cooked chicken in turn until they
are separated from the body and
then removing the remainder of the
meat from the bone in a random
way. This makes the meat look
messy and unappetizing and it is
also very uneconomical.

A chicken has natural breaks and
divisions in its body structure and
if you know exactly where to cut,
the joints will separate easily.

Always allow a cooked chicken to
relax for 5 minutes before starting
to carve. This will ease carving and
give the chicken juices a chance to
settle. Use a carving fork to steady
the bird. Insert the fork into one side
of the chicken and start to carve on
the opposite side. Insert the carving
knife between the leg and the body,
and ease the blade down until you
can feel the ball and socket joint.
Cut through the small piece of
sinew, removing the thigh and
drumstick in one piece. Turn the
chicken and repeat for the other
side (see illustration D).

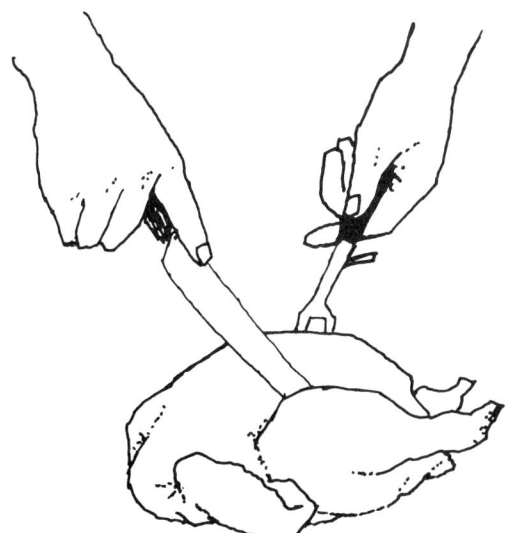

D

Next remove the wings. Cut along a line from the wishbone down through the ball and socket joint, cutting right through to separate the wing. Repeat with the other wing (see illustration E).

E

9

Now insert the knife behind the wishbone and slice off the front of the breast in even slices. Continue until all the meat has been removed from the carcass in neat pieces (see illustration F).

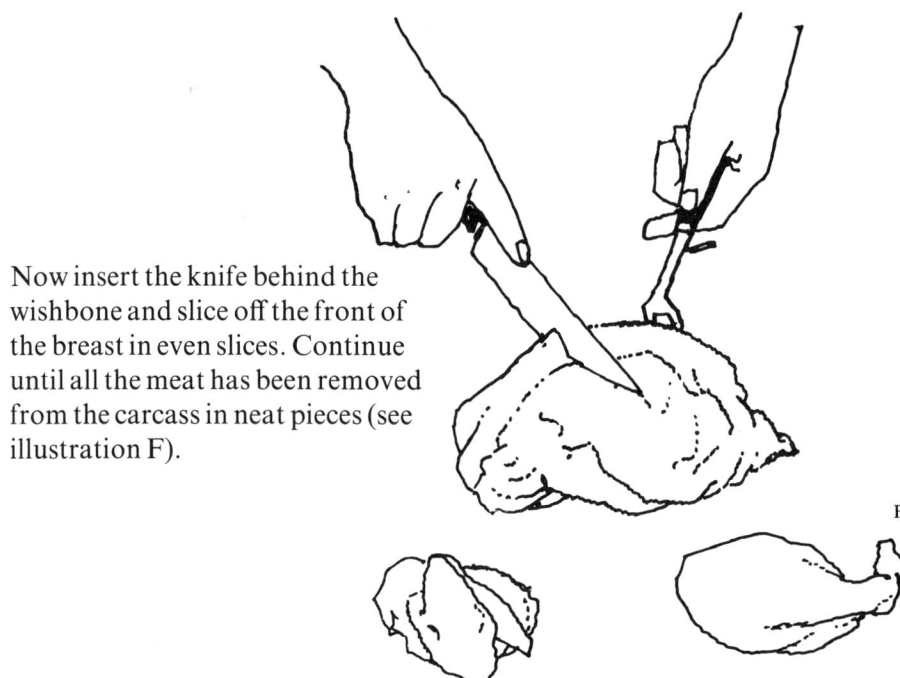

F

10

Weights and measures

All ingredient quantities are given in British Standard measurements, and the appropriate American measures for each ingredient follow at the foot of every recipe. Note that American spoon measures are smaller than British spoons:

1 British teaspoon equals $1\frac{1}{4}$ American teaspoons

1 British tablespoon equals $1\frac{1}{4}$ American tablespoons

The following metric equivalents apply for measuring ingredients, but note that metric measures are always given as convenient round figures and are only approximate equivalents. When converting large quantities one obtains slightly less of the finished product than when using ounces and pounds.

1 oz is taken as 25gm
4 oz are taken as 100gm
8 oz are taken as 225gm
1 lb is taken as 450gm

1 teaspoon is taken as 5ml
1 tablespoon is taken as 20ml
$\frac{1}{4}$ pint is taken as 150ml
$\frac{1}{2}$ pint is taken as 300ml
1 pint is taken as 600ml
2 pints are taken as 1 litre

Equivalent oven temperatures

250°F	Mark $\frac{1}{2}$	130°C
275°F	Mark 1	140°C
300°F	Mark 2	150°C
325°F	Mark 3	170°C
350°F	Mark 4	180°C
375°F	Mark 5	190°C
400°F	Mark 6	200°C
425°F	Mark 7	220°C
450°F	Mark 8	230°C

Abbreviations

teasp—teaspoon
tbsp—tablespoon
dessertsp—dessertspoon

All recipes that are marked with a star * are particularly suitable for freezing.

Chicken for starters

A starter can be the most appetizing part of a meal, livening up the taste buds for the courses that are to follow. It is important that a first course should be tasty, colourful and have an interesting texture, however light or substantial it might be.

There are many soups and hors d'oeuvres that can be based on chicken, both hot and cold.

The following recipes for chicken starters use both raw and cooked chicken, and some of them are ideal for using up chicken leftovers.

*Chicken and tomato soup

Serves 4

1 large chicken joint
1½ pints water
bay leaf
1 small onion, stuck with a clove
1½ oz butter
1½ oz flour
½ lb tomatoes, skinned, seeded
   and chopped
¼ pint double cream
salt and pepper

Put the chicken joint into a pan with
the water, bay leaf and onion.
Simmer for 30 minutes. Remove the
chicken joint from the liquid and
allow to cool. Melt the butter in a
pan and stir in the flour. Cook for 1
minute. Gradually add the strained
stock. Bring to the boil. Add the
chopped tomato and simmer for
10 minutes. Remove the flesh from
the cooked chicken joint and chop
finely. Add the chicken, cream and
seasoning to the soup and heat
through.

(American: 1¾ cups water, 3 tbsp
butter, 3 tbsp flour, ½ cup heavy
cream)

*Chicken and cucumber soup

Serves 4

*Special chicken soup packs can be
bought in most supermarkets.
Alternatively, use loose chicken
giblets.*

1 chicken soup pack
1½ pints water
1½ oz butter
½ large cucumber, peeled and grated
1 oz flour
¼ pint double cream
salt and pepper
thin slices of cucumber

Put the soup pack into a pan with
the water. Simmer for ½ hour. Strain
the stock. Melt the butter in a pan.
Add the grated cucumber and
sweat for 5 minutes. Stir in the flour
and cook for 1 minute. Gradually
add the strained stock. Bring to the
boil and simmer for 10 minutes.
Stir in the cream and seasoning and
reheat gently. Serve garnished with
slices of cucumber.

(American: 3½ cups water, 3 tbsp
butter, 2 tbsp flour, ½ cup cream)

*Avocado and chicken soup

Serves 4

1 chicken soup pack (see chicken
   and cucumber soup)
1½ pints water
salt and pepper
1 large ripe avocado
¼ pint double cream
chopped parsley

Put the soup pack into a pan with
the water. Simmer for 30 minutes.
Strain the stock. Cut the avocado in
half and remove the stone. Peel
thinly, taking care not to remove

too much of the dark green colouring. Chop the avocado and mix with half the strained stock. Push through a sieve or blend in a liquidizer until smooth. Put into a pan with the remaining stock and the cream. Bring just to the boil and season to taste. Serve either hot or chilled and garnished with chopped parsley.

(American: $3\frac{1}{2}$ cups water, $\frac{1}{2}$ cup heavy cream)

Chicken and cream cheese mousse

Serves 4–6

This tasty savoury mousse only takes a few minutes to make, so it is ideal if you are in a hurry. The chive flavoured cream cheese gives it a smooth creamy texture and a delicious flavour.

1 can consomme
4 oz chopped cooked chicken
3 oz packet rich full fat soft cheese
   with chives
salt and pepper

Put all the ingredients into the liquidizer and blend until smooth. Alternatively, mix all the ingredients well and push through a sieve. Pour into small cocotte dishes and chill until set. Serve with fingers of hot toast.

(American: $\frac{1}{3}$ cup cream cheese with chives)

Chicken and cheese pate

Serves 4
8 oz cottage cheese
1 onion, grated
1 tbsp chopped parsley
celery salt
ground black pepper
4 oz cooked chicken, finely chopped
1 oz chopped toasted nuts

Sieve the cottage cheese into a bowl. Add the grated onion, chopped parsley, celery salt and pepper to taste. Stir in the chicken. Put into a shallow dish and smooth level. Sprinkle the surface with chopped toasted nuts. Chill for 2 hours.

(American: 1 cup cottage cheese, 2 tbsp chopped toasted nuts)

Chicken avocado vinaigrette

Serves 4
6 oz cooked chicken
6 tbsp French dressing
1 tbsp chopped parsley
1 ripe avocado pear
1 small onion, sliced thinly
paprika

Pull the cooked chicken into small pieces. Put into a bowl and stir in the French dressing and chopped parsley. Cut the avocado in half lengthways. Remove the stone. Peel the avocado thinly and cut the flesh into slices. Stir into the chicken mixture until well coated in the dressing. Divide amongst 4 small plates and top with onion rings and a sprinkling of paprika. Serve with brown bread and butter.

Chicken nicoise

Serves 4

This is a meaty alternative to the traditional Salade nicoise, *and is suitable for serving as a light main meal in summer. If you can, buy smoked chicken. It lends a particularly delicious flavour to this dish.*

2 chicken breasts, fresh or smoked (see below)
white wine
salt and pepper
1 small lettuce, shredded
3 tomatoes, cut into sections
1 small onion, thinly sliced
2 oz black olives, pitted
French dressing

Smoked chicken does not require cooking. If you are using unsmoked chicken, put the breasts into a shallow pan. Add sufficient white wine to cover and seasoning to taste. Cover the pan and simmer gently until the chicken is just tender (approximately.30 minutes). Allow to cool.

Put the shredded lettuce into a bowl with the tomato, onion rings and black olives. Remove the chicken from the bone in large shreds and add to the other ingredients. Add sufficient French dressing to moisten.

(American : 4 tbsp black olives)

Chicken skordalia

Serves 4

This dish is based on the Greek skordalia *sauce made from egg yolks, garlic and olive oil.*

3 cloves garlic, crushed
2 egg yolks
salt and pepper
$\frac{1}{3}$ pint olive oil
2 oz fresh white breadcrumbs
juice and grated rind $\frac{1}{2}$ lemon
6 oz cooked chicken, pulled into strips

Beat the crushed garlic with the egg yolks. Gradually whisk in the oil, first drop by drop and then in a fine stream, as for making mayonnaise. Add the breadcrumbs, seasoning to taste, and the lemon rind and juice. Put the chicken strips onto a serving dish and spoon over the skordalia sauce. Chill thoroughly before serving.

(American : just under 1 cup olive oil, 4 tbsp breadcrumbs)

Curried chicken and prawns

Serves 4
$\frac{1}{4}$ pint mayonnaise (see p 59)
1 tbsp tomato puree
2 teasp curry powder

juice and grated rind ½ lemon
1 tbsp mango chutney
4 oz chopped cooked chicken
4 oz peeled prawns
4 poppadums

Mix the mayonnaise with the tomato puree, curry powder, lemon juice, rind and mango chutney. Add the chopped chicken and the prawns. Grill the poppadums lightly on both sides until puffed and golden – take care that they do not burn. Top each poppadum with the curried chicken and prawn mixture. Serve immediately so that the poppadums are still crisp.

(American: ½ cup mayonnaise)

Chilled spiced chicken

Serves 4

This dish has a tangy, spicy flavour without being as hot as a curry.

1 onion, chopped
1 crushed clove garlic
2 tbsp oil
½ teasp ground ginger
14 oz can tomatoes
1 tbsp tomato puree
1 teasp Worcester sauce
salt and pepper
½ lb lean boned chicken, in strips
1 tbsp preserved stem ginger,
    chopped

Fry the chopped onion and the garlic gently in oil. Add the ground

ginger, canned tomatoes, tomato puree, Worcester sauce and seasoning to taste. Simmer for 20 minutes. Add the strips of chicken and the chopped stem ginger. Chill thoroughly before serving.

If the quantities are increased this dish can be served with rice as a main course.

(American: 1½ cups canned tomatoes)

*Chicken and sweetcorn quiches

Serves 6
12 oz shortcrust pastry
11 oz can sweetcorn kernels
½ pint single cream
3 eggs
salt and pepper
6 oz chopped cooked chicken
3 oz grated cheese

Line 6 small individual flan dishes with the shortcrust pastry. Prick the base and bake blind for 10 minutes. Drain the sweetcorn kernels and mix with the cream, beaten eggs, seasoning and chopped chicken. Pour into the pastry cases. Sprinkle with grated cheese. Bake at 375°F, Mark 5, for 30 minutes.

(American: 1¼ cups sweetcorn kernels, 1¼ cups light cream, ½ cup grated cheese)

Devilled chicken croutes

Serves 4

3 oz rich full fat soft cheese with
   garlic and herbs
salt and pepper
4 oz cooked chicken, finely minced
4 diagonal slices French bread

Beat the cream cheese until quite
soft. Add seasoning to taste and
the minced chicken. Toast the
French bread on one side only.
Spread the untoasted side with the
chicken and cream cheese mixture.
Put under the grill until golden
and bubbling.

This dish can also be served as a
supper snack, easy to eat with the
fingers.

(American: $\frac{1}{3}$ cup cream cheese
with garlic and herbs)

Chicken for the oven

This section has many recipes for whole roast chickens, as well as some for baked chicken portions and dishes such as hot souffles.

Basic roasting methods are given in the recipes but for the more detailed preparation of whole chicken, such as trussing, see the introduction.

Spiced lemon chicken

Serves 6

Lemon gives a tangy, refreshing flavour to chicken, and in this recipe cloves add extra spice.

2 lemons, quartered
1 large onion, coarsely chopped
3½ lb chicken
salt and pepper
1½ teasp mixed spice
8 cloves
butter

Push the lemon quarters and chopped onion into the centre of the chicken. Stand the chicken in a roasting tin. Rub with salt, pepper and mixed spice. Stud the chicken with cloves. Spread generously with butter. Roast at 375°F, Mark 5, for 1½ hours, basting occasionally.

Orange glazed chicken

Serves 4–6
3½ lb chicken
Sweet Bread Stuffing (see p 61)
salt and pepper
butter
4 tbsp marmalade

Stuff the chicken with the Sweet Bread Stuffing. Put the chicken into a roasting dish. Season and spread generously with butter. Roast for 1 hour at 375°F, Mark 5, basting frequently. Spread marmalade evenly over the chicken and return to the oven for a further ½ hour. Add a little grated orange rind and juice to the gravy.

Note : a coarse cut marmalade gives the best flavour for this recipe, rather than a jellied or fine cut marmalade.

Chicken with mixed fruit stuffing

Serves 4–6

The prunes for the stuffing are plumped in tea, which adds an interesting and unusual flavour.

6 oz prunes
½ pint hot strained black tea
6 dessert apples, preferably the red skinned variety
1 onion, chopped
3½ lb chicken
butter
salt and pepper
2 tbsp cranberry jelly
juice ½ lemon

Soak the prunes in the hot tea until well plumped. Halve, core and chop 2 of the apples. Mix with half the drained prunes and the onion. Stuff into the centre of the chicken. Put the chicken into a roasting dish and spread generously with butter. Season with salt and pepper. Roast for 1½ hours at 375°F, Mark 5. Meanwhile, core the remaining apples. Chop the remaining prunes and mix with the cranberry jelly and lemon juice. Stand the apples filled with the prune mixture around the chicken for the last 20 minutes cooking time.

(American: $1\frac{1}{4}$ cups tea)

Corn bread chickens

Serves 6

Poussins are an excellent choice for a dinner party: gauging portions is simplified, and the cooked chickens look impressive.

1 onion, chopped
6 oz butter
4 oz sausagemeat
1 can sweetcorn kernels, drained
3 oz breadcrumbs
1 teasp mixed herbs
salt and pepper
2 tbsp chopped parsley
1 egg
4 tbsp cranberry jelly
grated rind and juice 1 orange
6 poussins

Fry the chopped onion gently in $\frac{1}{3}$ of the butter. Mix with the sausagemeat, drained sweetcorn, breadcrumbs, herbs, seasoning, chopped parsley and beaten egg.

Fill the poussins with the stuffing and truss so that they keep their shape during cooking. Stand the poussins in a roasting tin. Spread with the remaining butter and season with salt and pepper. Roast

at 375°F, Mark 5, for 45 minutes. Heat the cranberry jelly with the orange juice and rind and spoon over the poussins. Return to the oven for a further 20 minutes. Garnish with watercress and serve with extra cranberry jelly.

(American: $\frac{3}{4}$ cup butter, 1 cup sweetcorn kernels, $\frac{2}{3}$ cup bread-crumbs)

Savoury chicken roulade

Serves 6–8

A boned chicken makes it easy to slice and serve, and little of it is wasted. This dish is equally good served hot or cold.

$3\frac{1}{2}$ lb chicken, boned (see below)
Chestnut and Apricot Stuffing
    (see p 61)
butter
salt and pepper
$\frac{1}{4}$ pint red wine
$\frac{1}{4}$ pint orange juice
2 tbsp brown sugar

If you give your butcher advance warning he will bone the chicken for you, saving you time and effort.

Spread the boned chicken out, flesh side uppermost. Put the chestnut and apricot stuffing onto the chicken, and remould the chicken around the stuffing. Either secure the bird with small metal skewers, or, preferably, sew up with strong cotton or string. Put the chicken roulade into a roasting tin. Spread generously with butter and season to taste. Roast at 375°F, Mark 5, for 1 hour. Meanwhile, put the red wine, orange juice and brown sugar into a pan and reduce by half. Spoon over the chicken roulade and return to the oven for a further 30 minutes. Serve cut into thick slices with the glaze spooned over.

(American: $\frac{2}{3}$ cup red wine, $\frac{2}{3}$ cup orange juice)

*Chicken saltimbocca

Serves 4

This is a tasty variation on the popular Italian dish, saltimbocca, made with veal.

4 boned chicken breasts
salt and pepper
2 oz butter
1 teasp dried sage
4 slices smoked ham
4 slices Gruyere cheese
8 oz can tomatoes
1 tbsp tomato puree
1 clove garlic, crushed

Put the chicken breasts into a shallow ovenproof dish. Season to taste and top with knobs of butter. Sprinkle with sage. Bake at 375°F, Mark 5, for 10 minutes. Top each chicken breast with a slice of ham and a slice of cheese. Mix the canned tomatoes with the tomato puree and

garlic and spoon round the chicken. Bake for a further 30 minutes, until the cheese is bubbling and golden.

(American: 4 tbsp butter, $\frac{3}{4}$ cup canned tomatoes)

*Normandy chicken

Serves 4
2 cooking apples
2 oz raisins
4 tbsp honey
5 tbsp cider
salt and pepper
4 chicken portions

Peel, core and slice the apples. Put into a shallow ovenproof dish with the raisins, honey, cider, seasoning and chicken portions. Cover and cook at 375°F, Mark 5, for 45 minutes. Spoon the honey and cider juices over the chicken during cooking.

(American: 4 tbsp raisins)

*Tasty bake chicken

Serves 4
4 chicken drumsticks
4 tbsp flour
2 tbsp chopped parsley
1 teasp salt
$\frac{1}{2}$ teasp ground black pepper
1 teasp dried tarragon
beaten egg
3 oz butter
2 tbsp oil
2 bananas, cut into wedges

Skin the chicken drumsticks. Mix the flour, chopped parsley, salt, ground pepper and tarragon. Dip the chicken drumsticks into beaten egg, and then into the flour mixture, making sure that each drumstick is evenly coated. Chill for 1 hour. Heat the butter and oil in a shallow ovenproof dish until bubbling. Add the drumsticks and spoon over the hot fat. Bake at 400°F, Mark 6, for 35 minutes. Add the pieces of banana and return to the oven for a further 10 minutes.

(American: 6 tbsp butter)

*Baked chicken with ratatouille

Serves 4
1 onion, sliced
3 tbsp oil
14 oz can tomatoes
1 tbsp tomato puree
4 courgettes, sliced
1 medium size aubergine, chopped
1 clove garlic, crushed
salt and pepper
1 teasp oregano
4 chicken portions
melted butter or oil
3 oz grated cheese

Fry the onion gently in the oil. Add the canned tomatoes, tomato puree, courgettes, aubergine, garlic, seasoning and oregano. Simmer for 20 minutes. Put the ratatouille into a

shallow ovenproof dish and lay the chicken portions on top. Brush with melted butter or oil and bake at 375°F, Mark 5, for 30 minutes. Sprinkle with the grated cheese and return to the oven for a further 15 minutes. Serve piping hot with a crisp green salad.

Note: for convenience and speed canned or frozen ratatouille can be used instead of making your own. Add a little extra seasoning and garlic if you use a prepared ratatouille.

(American: 1½ cups canned tomatoes, ½ cup grated cheese)

*Moussaka chicken

Serves 4–6

This is a good recipe for using up cooked chicken.

½ lb cooked chicken
1 onion, sliced
4 tbsp oil
1 clove garlic, crushed
6 tomatoes, sliced
2 tbsp tomato puree
salt and pepper
½ pint natural yogurt
2 eggs
4 oz grated cheese

Pull the cooked chicken into small pieces. Fry the onion gently in the oil. Add the garlic and tomatoes and cook gently for 5 minutes. Add the tomato puree, seasoning and chicken. Spoon into a shallow ovenproof dish. Mix the yogurt with the beaten eggs and half the cheese. Spoon over the chicken and sprinkle the remaining cheese over the top. Bake at 375°F, Mark 5, for 40 minutes.

(American: $1\frac{1}{4}$ cups yogurt, $\frac{2}{3}$ cup grated cheese)

*Chicken and leek pie

Serves 6
$\frac{1}{2}$ a cooked chicken
3 leeks, sliced
2 onions, sliced
2 oz butter
salt and pepper
1 lb shortcrust pastry

beaten egg
$\frac{1}{4}$ pint soured cream

Remove the chicken flesh from the bone in large pieces. Fry the leeks and onions gently in butter. Mix with the pieces of chicken and season to taste. Roll out the pastry and use half to line a shallow pie dish. Fill with the chicken and vegetable mixture and cover with the remaining pastry, pinching the edges to seal. Glaze with beaten egg and make a hole in the top for the air to escape. Bake at 400°F, Mark 6, for 40 minutes. Remove from the oven and using a small funnel, pour the soured cream into the centre hole in the pie crust. Serve immediately.

(American: 4 tbsp butter, $\frac{1}{2}$ cup soured cream)

Chicken
for the pot

One of the most effortless ways of cooking chicken, and one of the most delicious, is in a casserole or stew. Boiling fowl is ideal for this prolonged, moist method of cooking, and it is inexpensive.

When stewing or casseroling always make sure that there is sufficient liquid to allow for any evaporation during cooking. Choose a casserole or pan with a well fitting lid, so that there is the minimum loss of moisture and flavour. The base of the pan should be very thick so that the ingredients do not stick and burn.

Chicken casseroles and stews give you the chance to be adventurous with flavours and to combine unusual ingredients. The following recipes give a few ideas for cooking chicken in a pot.

*Chicken paprika

Serves 4
2 onions, sliced
3 tbsp oil
4 chicken joints
1–2 tbsp paprika, according to
    taste
2 tbsp tomato puree
14 oz can tomatoes
$\frac{1}{4}$ pint stock
1 tbsp brown sugar
soured cream

Fry onion gently in oil. Add chicken joints and fry until lightly golden. Stir in paprika and cook for 1 minute. Add the tomato puree, canned tomatoes, stock and brown sugar. Season to taste. Cover and simmer for 1 hour. Top the chicken paprika with a little soured cream. Serve with noodles and crisp green salad, a refreshing contrast to the hot, spiciness of this dish.

(American: 1$\frac{1}{2}$ cups canned tomatoes, $\frac{2}{3}$ cup stock)

*Sweet sour chicken

Serves 4
4 chicken breasts
juice of 1 lemon
2 tbsp brown sugar
1 onion, finely chopped
1 can crushed pineapple
2 tbsp marmalade
1 green pepper, chopped
$\frac{1}{2}$ pint stock
$\frac{1}{4}$ teasp ground ginger
salt and pepper
1 tbsp soy sauce

Prick chicken breasts all over with a cocktail stick or fine skewer. Put into a shallow casserole and spoon over the lemon juice and brown sugar. Cover and refrigerate for 2 hours. Tip off any liquid from the chicken and put into a pan with the other ingredients. Bring to the boil and simmer for 10 minutes. Transfer the chicken to a baking dish and pour the sweet sour sauce over. Cover and cook at 375°F, Mark 5, for 45 minutes. Serve with bean sprouts.

(American: 1$\frac{1}{4}$ cups stock)

*Chicken and beer casserole

Serves 6
2 large onions, sliced
2 oz butter
2 tbsp flour
$\frac{3}{4}$ pint beer
$\frac{1}{2}$ pint stock
salt and pepper
6 chicken joints
$\frac{1}{4}$ lb button mushrooms
12 small cocktail sausages
croutons of fried bread

Fry the onions gently in the butter in a large casserole. Stir in the flour and cook for 1 minute. Add the beer and stock gradually, and bring to the boil. Season to taste. Add the

25

chicken joints. Cover the casserole and cook at 350°F, Mark 4, for 1 hour. Add the mushrooms and cocktail sausages and return to the oven, covered, for a further ½ hour. Serve garnished with the croutons of fried bread.

(American: 4 tbsp butter, 1⅔ cups beer, 1¼ cups stock)

*Normandy chicken casserole

Serves 6
4 oz prunes
1¼ pints cider
6 chicken drumsticks
seasoned flour
2 oz butter
grated rind ½ lemon
2 red skinned apples, cored and
   sliced
3 tbsp soured cream

Soak the prunes in half the cider for 4 hours. Dust the chicken drum-sticks in seasoned flour. Fry on all sides in butter until lightly golden. Put into a casserole with the soaked prunes and the remaining cider. Add the lemon rind. Cover the casserole and cook at 325°F, Mark 3, for 1½ hours. Add the cored and sliced apples and return to the oven for a further 30 minutes. Stir in the soured cream just before serving.

(American: 3 cups cider, 4 tbsp butter)

*Chicken and cabbage hotpot

Serves 4
1 small cabbage (see below)
1 onion, sliced
a few cloves
salt and pepper
4 tbsp golden syrup
2 tbsp vinegar
4 chicken joints
stock

Red or white cabbage can be used for this dish. If white cabbage is used, cook for only 2 hours.

Shred the cabbage finely. Put half the cabbage into a casserole with the onion, cloves, salt and pepper, golden syrup and vinegar. Top with the chicken joints and the remaining cabbage and flavourings. Add sufficient stock to come halfway up the depth of the ingredients. Cover with a lid and cook at 325°F, Mark 3, for 3 hours.

Chicken and vegetable hotpot

Serves 6

A selection of root vegetables makes this hotpot a hearty, satisfying meal for the family. Any leftover liquid can be used as the base for a tasty soup.

1 boiling fowl
2 onions, quartered
½ lb whole small carrots

26

½ lb swede, cut into chunks
½ lb potatoes, cut into chunks
2 leeks, cut into thick slices
4 oz dried kidney beans, soaked
     overnight
stock
bay leaf
few parsley stalks
salt and pepper

Put the boiling fowl into a large
saucepan with the prepared vegetables and add sufficient stock to
almost cover the chicken. Add the
bay leaf, parsley stalks and
seasoning. Cover the pan and
simmer for 1½–2 hours, until the
chicken is tender. Cut the chicken
into serving portions and serve with
the vegetables, moistened with a
little of the cooking liquid.

If liked, the cooking liquid can be
thickened to make a sauce. Small
dumplings can also be added to the
pan for the last 20 minutes' cooking.

Pickled chicken

Serves 6

*This dish could well be called
'soused' chicken, as the various
ingredients are similar to those used
for preparing soused herrings.*

3 lb boiling chicken
2 pints water
4 oz sea salt
4 bay leaves
2 teasp crushed peppercorns

2 teasp crushed juniper berries
4 tbsp brown sugar
½ pint vinegar
1 onion, sliced
1 carrot, sliced
¼ pint soured cream

Put the prepared chicken into a deep
ovenproof dish with all the
ingredients, apart from the soured
cream. Cover and refrigerate for
3 days. Put the chicken in its dish
into the oven, and cook covered at
325°F, Mark 3, for 1½ hours. Allow
the chicken to cool slightly, and
then remove all the meat from the
carcass in strips. Reduce the
cooking liquid by half. Stir in the
soured cream and the chicken and
heat through. Serve with rice.

(American: ½ cup sea salt, 1¼ cups
vinegar, ⅔ cup soured cream)

*Chicken bourguignon

Serves 4

4 poussins
3 oz butter
1 thick rasher streaky bacon,
     chopped
12 button onions
3 tbsp flour
½ pint stock
¾ pint red wine
salt and pepper
4 oz button mushrooms

Brown the poussins on all sides in
the butter. Put the baby chickens

into a casserole. Add the chopped bacon and button onions to the fat remaining in the pan and cook for a few minutes. Stir in the flour and cook for 1 minute. Gradually add the stock and wine and season to taste. Bring to the boil and pour over the poussins. Cover the casserole and cook at 350°F, Mark 4, for 1 hour. Add the mushrooms to the casserole and cook for a further 30 minutes. Sprinkle with chopped parsley before serving.

(American: 6 tbsp butter, 1¼ cups stock, 1⅔ cups red wine)

Coq au vin

Serves 4–6

This dish is based on the traditional coq au vin *recipe, but uses a whole chicken rather than chicken portions.*

3–3½ lb chicken

Six Herb Stuffing (see p 59)
2 oz butter
3 tbsp flour
¾ pint stock
¾ pint red wine
12 small button onions
4 oz button mushrooms
toast croutons

Fill the centre of the chicken with the Six Herb Stuffing. Brown on all sides in butter in a large casserole. Remove the chicken to a plate. Stir the flour into the fat in the casserole and cook for 1 minute. Gradually add the stock and red wine. Return the chicken to the casserole, together with the button onions. Cover and cook at 350°F, Mark 4, for 1 hour. Add the button mushrooms and return to the oven for a further 30 minutes. Serve garnished with toast croutons.

(American: 4 tbsp butter, 1¾ cups stock, 1¾ cups red wine)

Chicken for the frying pan

Chicken is equally suitable for both deep and shallow frying, depending on the cut and thickness of the chicken.

Small pieces of chicken such as boned chicken breasts and drumsticks can be coated and cooked in deep fat, as can thick chicken mixtures like the one used for chicken croquettes (see p 31).

All chicken joints can be shallow fried either in oil or in a mixture of oil and butter. Butter improves the flavour of the cooked chicken.

Most fried chicken is coated before cooking. When cooked the coating tends to be dry. To counteract this, all fried chicken dishes are best served with a sauce. For some suggestions, see pp 56-59.

Quick chicken creole

Serves 4
4 chicken joints
seasoned flour
4 tbsp oil
8 oz can tomatoes
4 tbsp bottled Thousand Island
    dressing

Dust the chicken joints in seasoned
flour. Fry gently in oil until golden
brown on all sides. Add the canned
tomatoes and the Thousand Island
dressing. Cover the pan and
continue cooking for 10 minutes.
Serve with rice.

(American: $\frac{3}{4}$ cup canned tomatoes)

Fried creamy chicken
with chestnuts

Serves 4
4 chicken joints
seasoned flour
2 oz butter
2 tbsp oil
1 onion, finely chopped
$\frac{1}{4}$ pint stock
$\frac{1}{4}$ pint milk
3 oz rich full fat or cream cheese
    with garlic and herbs
can of chestnuts (see below)

Freshly boiled chestnuts, soaked
dried chestnuts, or canned chestnuts
can be used in this recipe. Canned
chestnuts are listed in the ingredients, as they are generally the most
readily available. Canned chestnuts
are in a starchy liquid. Before using,
rinse it off carefully with hot water.

Dust the chicken joints in seasoned
flour. Heat the butter and oil in a
frying pan. Add the chicken and fry
until brown on all sides. Remove the
chicken from the pan. Add the
onion and fry for a few minutes.
Add the stock and return the
chicken to the pan. Cover and
simmer for 10–15 minutes. Blend
the milk and the cream cheese until
quite smooth. Stir into the pan and
add the whole chestnuts. Heat
through gently for a few minutes.

(American: 4 tbsp butter, $\frac{2}{3}$ cup
stock, $\frac{2}{3}$ cup milk, $\frac{1}{3}$ cup cheese,
1 cup chestnuts)

*Chicken in the basket

Serves 6

*This form of deep fried chicken has
gained great popularity as a pub
snack.*

6 chicken drumsticks
seasoned flour
1 egg
4 teasp French mustard
breadcrumbs
4 tbsp grated cheese
oil or fat for deep frying
watercress

Dust the chicken drumsticks in
seasoned flour. Beat the egg with

the mustard. Dip the drumsticks into the egg mixture and then coat evenly with breadcrumbs and grated cheese. Chill for 1 hour. Lower the coated drumsticks into a pan of hot deep fat or oil and fry until crisp, golden and tender – approximately 15 minutes, depending on the size of the drumsticks. Drain on absorbent paper. Serve in a napkin lined basket and garnish with watercress.

The drumsticks are particularly good served with Cider Barbecue Sauce (see p 59).

Freeze drumsticks coated but uncooked.

*Chicken and bacon croquettes

Serves 4

This is an excellent recipe for using up leftover cooked chicken and ham.

$\frac{1}{2}$ pint thick white sauce
2 egg yolks
6 oz cooked chicken, finely chopped
6 oz cooked bacon or ham, finely chopped
1 teasp mixed herbs
salt and pepper
flour
beaten egg
breadcrumbs
oil or fat for deep frying

Mix the thick white sauce with the egg yolks, chopped chicken and

ham, herbs and seasoning. Mould into 8 croquette shapes and dust in flour. Coat in beaten egg and crumbs. Chill for 1 hour so that the croquettes firm up and keep their shape. Lower into a pan of hot deep fat or oil and fry for about 8 minutes, until crisp and golden brown. Drain well and serve with a piquant sauce. Cranberry Sauce is ideal (see p 57).

Freeze croquettes uncooked.

(American: $1\frac{1}{4}$ cups thick white sauce)

Spatchcock chicken

Serves 2

This recipe can only be for 2 people as it is impossible to cook more than 2 small chickens at the same time in one pan.

2 poussins
seasoned flour
2 oz butter
2 tbsp oil
1 onion, sliced
4 oz mushrooms, sliced
4 tomatoes, chopped
$\frac{1}{4}$ pint red wine
1 teasp oregano
juice $\frac{1}{2}$ lemon

Your butcher will prepare the poussins if you ask him in advance. The breastbone is first removed, using poultry shears, and then the baby chicken is turned over and flattened with a meat mallet or rolling pin. The chickens are then kept flat by threading 2 skewers diagonally through each one.

Dust the spatchcock chickens in seasoned flour. Heat the butter and oil in a large frying pan. Add the chickens and fry on both sides until nicely browned. Remove the chickens from the pan. Add the sliced onion and fry gently for a few minutes. Add the mushrooms, tomatoes, red wine, oregano and lemon juice and bring to the boil. Return the chickens to the pan. Cover and simmer gently for 10 minutes. Serve with buttered noodles.

(American. 4 tbsp butter, ⅔ cup red wine)

*Chicken maryland

Serves 4
4 chicken breasts
seasoned flour
beaten egg
golden breadcrumbs
oil or fat for deep frying
canned creamed sweetcorn
grilled bacon rolls
fried wedges of banana
watercress

Dust the chicken breasts in seasoned flour. Dip into the beaten egg and coat evenly in breadcrumbs. Chill for 1 hour to set the crumb coating. Lower the coated chicken portions into a pan of hot deep fat or oil, and fry until crisp, golden and tender. Test the meat with a fine skewer. The cooking time will depend on the size of the chicken breasts. Drain well on absorbent paper.

Serve the cooked chicken on a bed of hot sweetcorn and garnish with bacon rolls, wedges of fried banana, and watercress.

Note: for a change in flavour, the chicken portions can be coated in dry stuffing mix instead of bread-crumbs.

Freeze cooked chicken only.

Chinese style stir fried chicken

Serves 4

This dish is ideal when you are in a hurry. Once all the ingredients are prepared, it only takes 15 minutes to cook.

4 boned chicken breasts
2 oz butter
2 tbsp oil
2 onions, sliced
1 leek, cut into matchstick strips
3 stems celery, cut into matchstick strips
1 green pepper, cut into strips
4 water chestnuts, sliced
1 can bean sprouts

2 teasp sugar
1 tbsp soy sauce
salt and pepper

Cut the chicken meat into thin strips. Heat the butter and oil in a large frying pan. Add the strips of chicken and fry quickly until golden brown. Test that the chicken is tender. Add all the remaining ingredients and fry quickly for 3–4 minutes, stirring continuously. All the vegetables should still be quite crisp. Serve with extra soy sauce.

(American: 4 tbsp butter, 1 cup canned bean sprouts)

Chicken with orange and sherry sauce

Serves 4
4 chicken breasts
seasoned flour
1 onion, grated
2 oz butter
3 tbsp coarse cut marmalade
$\frac{1}{4}$ pint sherry
2 tbsp chopped parsley

Dust the chicken breasts in seasoned flour. Fry the grated onion gently in the butter until soft. Add the chicken breasts and fry gently until golden brown on both sides. Stir in the marmalade, sherry and chopped parsley, and simmer very gently for 10–15 minutes, until the chicken is tender. The liquid in the pan reduces during cooking and the chicken takes on an attractive gloss. Serve with a crisp chicory salad.

(American: 4 tbsp butter, $\frac{2}{3}$ cup sherry)

*Pollo sorpresa

Serves 4

This dish is sometimes called Chicken Kiev. The preparation is complicated, so it is best to ask your butcher to prepare the chicken pieces for you.

4 boned chicken breasts with
    wing bones attached
4 oz butter
grated rind and juice $\frac{1}{2}$ lemon
2 cloves garlic, crushed
2 tbsp chopped parsley
1 teasp dried tarragon
seasoned flour
beaten egg
breadcrumbs
oil or fat for deep frying

The flavoured butter must be prepared in advance, and if more convenient it can be kept for a few days in the freezer or the ice compartment of the refrigerator. Soften the butter and beat with the lemon rind and juice, crushed garlic, parsley and tarragon. Season to taste. Shape into a rectangle, wrap in greaseproof paper, and chill until firm. Divide into four equal portions for use.

To assemble the pollo sorpresa:
batten the breast part of the chicken pieces between dampened sheets of greaseproof paper. When ready, place a portion of flavoured butter onto each flattened chicken breast. Roll up neatly, pressing together to enclose the butter and leaving the wing bone protruding at one end. Secure with cocktail sticks. Dust in seasoned flour and coat in egg and breadcrumbs. Chill for 1–2 hours, or overnight if possible.

Lower the coated chicken breasts into a pan of hot fat or oil and deep fry for about 10 minutes, until the chicken is golden brown. Remove from the fat and drain on absorbent paper. Carefully remove the cocktail sticks and serve immediately with French fried potatoes and a green salad. Before eating the chicken breasts must be pierced very carefully so that the hot butter does not spurt out.

Note: the chicken breasts can be stuffed with chilled cubes of rich full fat soft cheese, either plain or flavoured, as an alternative to the flavoured butter.

Freeze prepared chicken breasts uncooked.

(American: $\frac{1}{2}$ cup butter)

Chicken for the grill

Chicken is very suitable for cooking by direct heat, whether under a grill or on the open heat of a barbecue. Whichever method is used, the chicken benefits from being basted regularly to keep it moist.

All the recipes given in this section specify using the grill, but all can easily be adapted for a barbecue.

The sauces and savoury butters given in the last section of the book are ideal for serving with grilled and barbecued chicken.

Chicken kebabs

Serves 6
4 boned chicken breasts
¼ pint natural yogurt
pinch mixed spice
¼ teasp turmeric
2 teasp Worcester sauce
12 button mushrooms
6 rashers bacon, halved and formed
    into rolls
oil
salt and pepper

Cut the boned chicken meat into even sized pieces, about 1 in square. Put into a shallow dish with the yogurt, mixed spice, turmeric and Worcester sauce. Cover and chill for 1 hour. Remove the pieces of chicken from the yogurt marinade, and thread onto kebab skewers, alternating the pieces of chicken with button mushrooms and bacon rolls. Brush with oil and put on the rack of the grill pan. Cook for 5 minutes. Turn the kebabs and spoon over some of the yogurt marinade. Continue cooking under the grill for a further 5 minutes, or until the pieces of chicken are tender. Serve with rice.

(American: ⅔ cup yogurt)

Simple curried chicken

Serves 4
4 chicken joints
curry paste
salt and pepper
juice 1 lemon
oil

Spread each chicken joint generously with curry paste. Put into a shallow dish and season with salt, pepper and lemon juice. Cover and chill for 2 hours. Put the chicken joints onto the rack of the grill pan and baste with oil. Cook until crispy brown. Turn the chicken joints and continue cooking until the chicken is tender right through, basting occasionally with more oil.

The grilled curried chicken can be eaten either hot or cold. Serve with a bowl of natural yogurt, mango chutney and a crisp salad.

Garlic and cream chicken

Serves 4

The quantity of garlic in this recipe is quite large – if you prefer, use only one clove.

2 cloves garlic, crushed
juice ½ lemon
¼ pint soured cream
pinch grated nutmeg
1 small onion, grated
1 teasp paprika
1 teasp mixed herbs
salt and pepper
4 chicken joints

Mix the first eight ingredients together. Put the chicken joints into a shallow dish and spoon over the garlic and cream marinade. Cover and chill overnight. Remove the chicken from the marinade and place on the rack of the grill pan. Baste with the marinade and grill until crispy brown. Turn the chicken joints and baste once again with the marinade. Continue cooking until the chicken is tender right through.

The chicken can be eaten either hot or cold, and it is ideal for a picnic.

(American: $\frac{2}{3}$ cup soured cream)

Chicken limey

Serves 4

Chicken is enhanced by the flavour of citrus fruits, particularly limes. Fresh limes are expensive and often difficult to find, but lime juice cordial can be used quite successfully in this recipe.

4 chicken joints
4 tbsp lime juice cordial
1 tbsp fresh mint, chopped
salt and pepper
melted butter
2 oz flaked almonds

Make several incisions in the chicken joints with a sharp knife. Put into a shallow dish and spoon over the lime juice. Add the chopped mint and seasoning. Cover and chill for 1 hour. Remove the chicken from the dish and put onto the rack of the grill pan. Brush with melted butter and grill under a moderate

heat for about 10 minutes. Turn the chicken joints and brush with more melted butter. Continue grilling until the chicken is tender. Sprinkle with flaked nuts and return to the grill until the nuts start to brown. Serve either hot or cold.

This is another good chicken dish to choose for a picnic or outdoor meal.

(American: $\frac{1}{3}$ cup flaked nuts)

Barbecued apricot chicken

Serves 4

15 oz can apricot halves
1 tbsp soy sauce
1 tbsp honey
1 tbsp tomato puree
juice $\frac{1}{2}$ lemon
salt and pepper
4 chicken joints
oil

Strain the apricots (save the juice and use as the base for a fruit drink). Push the apricots through a sieve. Mix with the soy sauce, honey, tomato puree, lemon juice and seasoning. Brush the chicken joints with oil and part cook on one side under a preheated grill. Turn the chicken joints and spread with the apricot baste. Continue cooking under the grill until the chicken is cooked right through.

(American: $1\frac{1}{2}$ cups canned apricots)

Simple barbecued drumsticks

Serves 4
4 chicken drumsticks
3 tbsp tomato ketchup
1 tbsp soft brown sugar
2 teasp vinegar
2 teasp made mustard
½ teasp Tabasco sauce
salt and pepper
1 teasp mixed herbs
oil

Prick the drumsticks all over with a
cocktail stick or fine skewer. Put
into a shallow dish. Mix the
ketchup, brown sugar, vinegar,
mustard, Tabasco sauce, seasoning
and herbs. Spread the chicken
drumsticks with the barbecue baste.
Cover and chill for 2 hours. Put the
drumsticks onto the rack of the grill
pan and trickle over a little oil.
Grill under a moderate heat for 10
minutes. Turn the drumsticks and
spoon over any remaining barbecue
baste. Grill for a further 5–10
minutes, until the chicken is tender.
Serve with jacket potatoes and a
salad.

Skewered drumsticks

Serves 4

*A king-size version of the kebab – the
chicken joint is threaded onto the
skewer whole, brushed with a tasty
baste, and then grilled.*

4 chicken drumsticks
2 tbsp chutney
1 tbsp tomato puree
juice ½ lemon
1 tbsp vinegar
2 tbsp honey
salt and pepper

Thread each chicken drumstick
onto a kebab skewer. Mix the
chutney with the tomato puree,
lemon juice, vinegar, honey and
seasoning. Spread evenly over each
chicken drumstick. Balance across
the grill pan and cook under a
moderate heat for 6–8 minutes.
Turn the chicken drumsticks and
baste with any juices that drip into
the grill pan. Continue cooking until
the chicken drumsticks are tender.

Children will love these chicken
drumsticks rolled in chopped
peanuts after cooking. Try them
like this served cold.

Cheesy grilled chicken

Serves 4
4 poussins, prepared as for
    Spatchcock Chicken (see p 31)
French mustard, according to taste
melted butter
garlic salt
ground black pepper
4 slices Gruyere cheese

Spread the surface of the poussins
with French mustard. Put on the
rack of the grill pan and spoon over

melted butter to moisten. Grill under a moderate heat for 10 minutes. Season with garlic salt and ground black pepper and top each flattened poussin with a slice of cheese. Spoon over more melted butter and return to the grill for about 5 minutes, until the cheese is bubbling and golden. Eat while very hot.

Chicken and mushroom rarebits

Serves 4
4 oz chopped mushrooms
2 oz butter
1 onion, grated
6 oz cooked chicken, chopped
4 slices bread
3 oz rich full fat soft cheese
salt and pepper
4 oz grated cheese

Fry the chopped mushrooms gently with the grated onion in butter until soft. Stir in the chopped cooked chicken and keep warm. Toast the bread on one side only. Spread the untoasted side with rich full fat cheese. Pop under the grill until the cheese begins to melt. Top each slice with the mushroom and chicken mixture and sprinkle with grated cheese. Return to the grill until golden and bubbling.

(American: 4 tbsp butter, $\frac{1}{3}$ cup cream cheese)

Chicken avocado grills

Serves 4

If you can find a stockist, smoked chicken is best for this recipe. Otherwise use slices of roast chicken.

4 diagonal slices from a French loaf
butter
4 slices of smoked or roast chicken
1 avocado pear, stoned, peeled and
    thinly sliced
6 oz grated Cheddar cheese
sliced stuffed olives
parsley

Toast the slices of French bread lightly on both sides. Put a slice of chicken on top of each and cover with slices of peeled avocado. Top with a generous layer of grated cheese. Grill until the cheese melts. Garnish with sliced olives and parsley and serve immediately.

Chicken
for cold dishes

Chicken lends itself as well to cold dishes as to hot. The meat used can be either the leftovers from a whole cooked bird or chicken that is cooked specially to be served cold.

Many cold dishes are quite substantial and are suitable for serving all the year round, not just with salads in summer. If the weather is very cold, hot vegetables or baked garlic bread can be served as accompaniments.

The great advantage with cold chicken dishes, as with all prepared cold food, is that they can be prepared in advance, and they are ideal for buffets and supper parties. In fact many of the dishes improve in flavour by being prepared the night before.

*Chicken terrine

Serves 4
½ lb fat salt pork
1½ lb boned chicken
2 cloves garlic, crushed
2 tbsp chopped parsley
2 teasp mixed herbs
2 eggs
4 tbsp brandy
salt and pepper

Mince the pork and chicken together. Put the meats into a bowl and mix with the garlic, parsley, herbs, eggs, brandy and seasoning. Leave to stand in a cool place for 1 hour to allow the flavours to develop. Put into a greased loaf tin or terrine (if liked, the tin or terrine can be lined with rashers of streaky bacon). Stand the tin or terrine inside a larger roasting tin or dish, containing a 2 in depth of water. Cook at 300°F, Mark 2, for 1½ hours, covered with a lid or foil. Remove the lid or foil and continue the cooking for a further 30 minutes. Allow to cool with a weight on top. When quite cold, cover either with a layer of melted butter or aspic jelly, and decorate with bay leaves, juniper berries, etc.

Chicken tonnato

Serves 4
7½ oz can tuna fish
small can anchovy fillets
grated rind and juice ½ lemon
1 clove garlic, crushed
salt and pepper
½ pint homemade mayonnaise
   (see p 59)
1 small cooked chicken
2 tbsp capers
watercress

Put the canned tuna fish, including its oil, into a liquidizer with half the anchovy fillets, the lemon rind and juice, crushed garlic, salt and pepper, and mayonnaise. Blend until quite smooth. Alternatively, pound all these ingredients together in a mortar and pestle. Skin the chicken and remove all the flesh from the bone in even sized pieces. Put the chicken into a shallow serving dish and spoon over the tonnato sauce. Chill for 2 hours. Garnish with the remaining anchovy fillets, capers and watercress.

(American: ⅔ cup tuna fish, 1¼ cups homemade mayonnaise)

Chilled chicken curry

Serves 4

This spicy cold chicken is deliciously refreshing when the weather is hot, and with a rice salad it is an ideal dish to take on a picnic.

½ pint homemade mayonnaise
   (see p 59)
1½ tbsp curry powder
grated rind and juice ½ lemon

¼ pint soured cream
1 onion, grated
12 oz cooked chicken, chopped
2 oz sultanas
1 red skinned apple, cored and
    chopped
salt and pepper

Mix the mayonnaise with the curry powder, lemon rind and juice, soured cream and grated onion. Stir in the chicken, sultanas, apple and seasoning. Chill for at least 2 hours.

Serve with a rice salad and some of the usual curry accompaniments such as poppadums, mango chutney, coconut and lime pickles.

(American: 1¼ cups homemade mayonnaise, ⅔ cup soured cream, 2 cups chopped cooked chicken)

Hawaiian chicken salad

Serves 4
1 small ripe pineapple
½ lb cooked chicken, chopped
4 spring onions, chopped
¼ pint soured cream
4 tbsp homemade mayonnaise
    (see p 59)
2 oz pecan nuts, chopped
salt and pepper

Cut the pineapple in half lengthways, keeping the pine intact. Carefully scoop out the centre flesh from the pineapple and cut into pieces. Mix the chopped

pineapple with the chicken, spring onions, soured cream, mayonnaise, nuts and seasoning. Spoon into the pineapple shells.

(American: ⅔ cup soured cream, 4 tbsp chopped pecan nuts)

Chicken and lettuce dolmas

Serves 4
12 oz cooked chicken
4 oz smoked ham
1 small onion
1 clove garlic, crushed
3 hard-boiled eggs, chopped
3 tbsp cream
salt and pepper
8 large lettuce leaves
approximately ¼ pint French
    dressing
2 tbsp chopped parsley

Mince the cooked chicken, smoked ham and onion. Mix with the garlic, 2 of the chopped hard-boiled eggs, the cream and seasoning. Put a spoonful of the mixture into the centre of each lettuce leaf and fold over the lettuce parcel fashion, to enclose the filling. Stand the lettuce dolmas in a shallow dish. Mix the French dressing with the remaining chopped hard-boiled egg and the chopped parsley. Spoon over the lettuce dolmas.

(American: 2 cups cooked chicken, ⅔ cup cooked ham)

Chicken with guacamole

Serves 4

This can either be served with salad as a main meal or with fingers of brown bread and butter as a starter. As a starter it will serve 8 people.

2 ripe Carmel avocados
8 oz cream cheese
1 small onion, finely chopped
$\frac{1}{2}$ green pepper, finely chopped
$\frac{1}{4}$ teasp paprika
few drops Tabasco sauce
juice of $\frac{1}{2}$ lemon
1 clove garlic, crushed
salt
12 oz cooked chicken, pulled into
   strips

Mash the peeled and stoned avocados. Add the cream cheese, onion, pepper, paprika, Tabasco, lemon juice, garlic and salt. Beat until smooth. Stir in the pieces of chicken. Chill for 2 hours before serving.

(American: 1 cup cream cheese, 2 cups cooked chicken)

Chicken and bean sprout salad

Serves 4
12 oz cooked chicken, pulled into
   strips
2 tbsp soy sauce
juice $\frac{1}{2}$ lemon
$\frac{3}{4}$ lb bean sprouts

1 onion, sliced finely
4 oz button mushrooms, sliced
4 pieces stem ginger, chopped
French dressing
2 oz toasted flaked almonds

Put the chicken strips into a shallow dish and spoon over the soy sauce and lemon juice. Cover and chill for 2 hours. Stir the marinated chicken into the bean sprouts with the onion, mushrooms and ginger. Add sufficient French dressing to moisten. Sprinkle with toasted nuts.

(American: 2 cups cooked chicken, $\frac{2}{3}$ cup sliced mushrooms)

*Chicken ratatouille salad

Serves 6
1 onion, sliced
6 tbsp oil
2 aubergines, cut into cubes
6 courgettes, sliced
1 large green pepper, sliced
14 oz can tomatoes
2 tbsp tomato puree
2 cloves garlic, crushed
1 teasp oregano
salt and pepper
6 chicken drumsticks

Fry the sliced onion gently in the oil. Add the aubergines, courgettes, green pepper, tomatoes, tomato puree, garlic, oregano and salt and pepper. Bring to the boil. Add the chicken drumsticks. Cover the pan and simmer for $\frac{3}{4}$ hour. Allow to cool and then chill, preferably overnight. Serve with green salad.

(American: 1½ cups canned tomatoes)

Chicken Peter Heering

Serves 4–6

Peter Heering liqueur gives a very distinctive flavour to this jellied chicken dish.

½ pint chicken stock
1 tbsp gelatine
½ pint Peter Heering liqueur
few lemon slices
few mint leaves
4 cooked chicken breasts, boned
   and sliced
salt and pepper
lettuce leaves
tomato quarters

Heat the chicken stock gently with the gelatine until dissolved. Allow to cool and stir in the Peter Heering. When the jelly has become thick and syrupy, pour a little around the inside of a dampened 2 pint mould, to give an even coating. Garnish the semi-set jelly with lemon slices and mint. Allow to set. Fill jelly-lined mould with the pieces of cooked chicken and fill up with the remaining Peter Heering jelly. Chill to set. Unmould the set jelly onto a plate and garnish with lettuce leaves and quarters of tomato.

(American: 1¼ cups chicken stock, 1¼ cups Peter Heering liqueur)

Chicken with blue cheese and bacon sauce

Serves 4
4 chicken breasts, boned
¼ pint stock
¼ pint cream
salt and pepper
1 onion, finely chopped
2 egg yolks
4 oz Danish blue cheese, crumbled
4 rashers bacon, grilled crisply
pinch grated nutmeg

Cut the chicken breasts into strips. Put into a shallow pan with the stock and cream, seasoning and onion. Cover and simmer gently until the chicken is just tender. Drain the pieces of cooked chicken and put into a shallow dish. Beat the egg yolks and stir into the cooking liquid. Stir over a gentle heat until lightly thickened. Add the crumbled blue cheese and spoon over the chicken. Chill for 2 hours. Sprinkle with crumbled crisp bacon before serving. Serve with crusty French bread.

Chicken with peanut sauce

Serves 4
4 tbsp peanut butter
1 onion, grated

½ pint cream
salt and pepper
4 cooked chicken joints (see recipe)
onion rings
roasted peanuts, chopped

Soften the peanut butter and beat in the grated onion and cream (this can be done in the liquidizer). Add seasoning. If possible cook the chicken freshly and spoon the sauce over while the chicken is still warm. Make several slits in the chicken and spoon the peanut sauce over. Chill for at least 2 hours. Garnish with onion rings and peanuts.

(American: 1¼ cups cream)

Chicken veronique

Serves 4

This is a delicious way of combining chicken with fruit. Instead of cooked chicken joints, pieces of leftover chicken can be used.

4 chicken joints, poached in stock
    or wine
¼ pint homemade mayonnaise
    (see p 59)
¼ pint double cream, whipped
¼ pint white wine (see recipe)
1 clove garlic, crushed
grated rind and juice ½ lemon
salt and pepper
pinch grated nutmeg
6 oz green grapes

Skin the chicken joints and remove any excess bone. Put the chicken

into a shallow dish. Mix the mayonnaise with the double cream and the white wine (if the chicken joints have been cooked in wine, use the strained cooking liquid). Add the garlic, lemon rind and juice, seasoning and nutmeg. Spoon over the chicken. Cover and chill for 2 hours. Stir in the grapes, preferably skinned and depipped, keeping a few whole for garnishing the top.

(American: ⅔ cup homemade mayonnaise, ⅔ cup heavy cream, ⅔ cup white wine)

Spiced chicken in milk

Serves 4
1 small boiling chicken
1 teasp ground cloves
½ teasp ground cinnamon
½ teasp ground ginger
½ teasp ground cardamom
grated rind 1 lemon
1 clove garlic, crushed
2 pints milk
2 egg yolks
¼ pint cream
salt and pepper
wedges of lemon
few toasted nuts

Prick the boiling chicken all over with a fork. Mix the ground spices with the lemon rind and crushed garlic. Rub well into the surface of the chicken. Chill for 2 hours. Put the chicken into a saucepan with the milk. Cover and simmer about $1\frac{1}{4}$ hours, until the chicken is tender. Remove the chicken from its cooking liquid and allow to cool. Remove the meat from the carcass in even size pieces and put into a shallow dish. Measure $\frac{3}{4}$ pint of the cooking liquid and put into the top of a double saucepan. Beat the egg yolks with the cream and add to the liquid. Stir over the heat until the sauce has thickened lightly. Pour over the chicken and leave until quite cold. Garnish with wedges of lemon and toasted nuts.

(American: 5 cups milk, $\frac{2}{3}$ cup cream)

Jellied chicken with champagne

Serves 6
$\frac{1}{2}$ lb lambs liver
1 onion, grated
2 oz butter
1 clove garlic, crushed
$\frac{1}{2}$ lb sausagemeat
2 oz breadcrumbs
4 tbsp brandy
1 egg yolk
salt and pepper
$3\frac{1}{2}$ lb chicken
1 pint chicken stock
$\frac{1}{2}$ pint champagne
sachet of aspic jelly (to make up 1 pint)
fresh tarragon

Chop the lambs liver. Fry gently in butter with the grated onion for a few minutes. Mix with the garlic, sausagemeat, breadcrumbs, brandy, egg yolk and seasoning. Stuff the chicken with the liver mixture. Sew up the chicken with coarse cotton. Put into a deep pan. Add the stock and cover the pan. Simmer gently for $1\frac{1}{2}$ hours. Test that the chicken is tender. Remove the chicken and allow to cool. Pour the cooking liquid through a sieve. There should be $\frac{1}{2}$ pint. If necessary make up to $\frac{1}{2}$ pint with a little extra stock. Add the champagne and warm gently. Dissolve the aspic jelly crystals in the champagne liquid. Chill until the aspic becomes syrupy. Stand the chicken on a wire rack and spoon over the champagne aspic to give an even glaze. Chill overnight. Place on a serving dish and garnish with small sprigs of fresh tarragon.

(American: 4 tbsp butter, 4 tbsp breadcrumbs, $2\frac{1}{2}$ cups chicken stock, $1\frac{1}{4}$ cups champagne)

Foreign ways with chicken

Chicken is eaten in almost every country in the world, from the Sahara Desert to the Steppes of Russia.

The methods of cooking, however, vary enormously. It is sometimes cooked over an open fire, sometimes heavily spiced, and sometimes it is served with pasta or rice.

In this section I have given some interesting and unusual chicken recipes that can be made quite easily with ingredients that are readily available in this country.

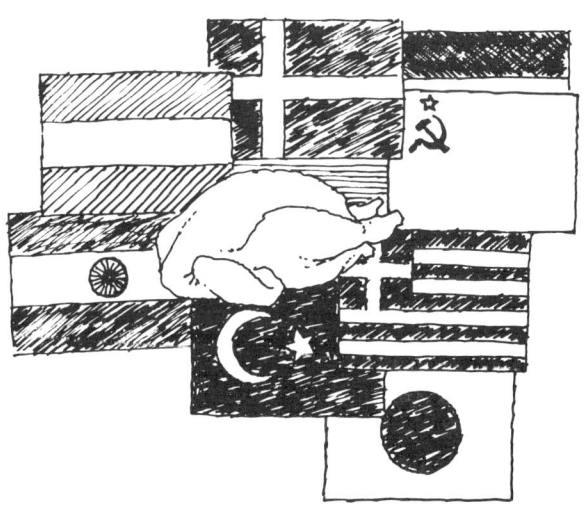

France:
Poulet saute vallee d'Auge

Serves 4
4 chicken joints
3 oz butter
2 tbsp oil
salt and pepper
4 tbsp Calvados or brandy
$\frac{1}{4}$ pint chicken stock
4 spring onions, finely chopped
2 stems celery, finely chopped
2 medium cooking apples, cored,
    peeled and chopped
2 tbsp chopped parsley
2 egg yolks
$\frac{1}{4}$ pint double cream
watercress

Heat 2 oz of the butter and the oil in a large frying pan. Add the chicken joints and brown on all sides. Remove the chicken to a plate. Tip off most of the fat, leaving about 1 tbsp. Return the chicken to the pan. Take the pan off the heat and add the Calvados or brandy and carefully set light to the pan. Shake gently to and fro until the flames die down. Add the stock and stir to dissolve the sediment. Melt the remaining butter in a small pan. Add the spring onions, celery, apples, parsley and seasoning, and cook gently, stirring, for 10 minutes. Add to the chicken in the frying pan and bring to the boil. Cover and simmer for about 30 minutes, until the chicken is tender. Remove the

cooked chicken to a serving dish and keep warm in the oven. Press the sauce through a sieve and skim off any fat. Put the sauce into a pan and stir over the heat until reduced and thick. Blend the egg yolks with the cream and stir into the sauce. Stir over a moderate heat for 2–3 minutes. Do not allow the sauce to boil. Season the sauce and spoon over the chicken. Garnish with watercress.

(American: 6 tbsp butter, $\frac{2}{3}$ cup stock, $\frac{2}{3}$ cup heavy cream)

*Fricassee de poulet

Serves 4
4 oz butter
4 chicken joints
salt and pepper
1 oz flour
1 pint chicken stock
bouquet garni
16 button onions
$\frac{1}{2}$ lb button mushrooms
2 egg yolks
$\frac{1}{4}$ pint double cream
chopped parsley

Heat the butter in a large frying pan. Add the chicken joints, season, and fry until brown on all sides. Remove the chicken to a plate. Stir the flour into the butter remaining in the pan and cook for 1 minute. Gradually add the stock. Bring to the boil, allow to thicken lightly and add the chicken, bouquet garni and button onions. Cover and simmer for 15 minutes. Add the button mushrooms and simmer for a further 15 minutes. Remove the bouquet garni, beat the egg yolks with the cream and gradually stir into the sauce. Heat through to thicken the sauce, but do not boil. Sprinkle with chopped parsley before serving.

(American: 4 tbsp butter, 2 tbsp flour, $2\frac{1}{2}$ cups stock, $1\frac{1}{2}$ cups button mushrooms, $\frac{2}{3}$ cup heavy cream)

Denmark:
Stegt kylling

Serves 4
$3\frac{1}{2}$ lb roasting chicken
$\frac{1}{4}$ lb softened butter
salt and pepper
large bunch parsley
1 oz butter
3 tbsp oil
$\frac{1}{4}$ pint stock
$\frac{1}{4}$ pint double cream

Spread the inside of the chicken with the softened butter. Season inside and out with salt and pepper and stuff the centre of the chicken with parsley. Truss so that the chicken holds its shape. Heat the butter and oil in a pan and brown the chicken on all sides. Put the chicken into a casserole. Tip off most of the fat from the pan, leaving about 1 tbsp.

Add the stock and heat to dissolve the sediment. Pour over the chicken. Cover the casserole and cook at 325°F, Mark 3, for $1\frac{1}{4}$ hours. Remove the chicken to a serving dish and keep warm. Skim any fat from the cooking juices. Add the cream and bring to the boil. Simmer until the sauce reduces and thickens. Adjust the seasoning. Serve the carved chicken with the cream sauce, cucumber and dill salad and boiled potatoes.

(American: $\frac{1}{2}$ cup softened butter, 2 tbsp butter, $\frac{2}{3}$ cup stock, $\frac{2}{3}$ cup heavy cream)

Russia:
Kurnik

Serves 4–6
1 small boiling fowl
2 onions, sliced
2 stems celery, chopped
bay leaf
1 teasp crushed peppercorns
2 pints water
3 oz butter
$\frac{1}{2}$ lb button mushrooms, sliced
2 tbsp chopped parsley
juice $\frac{1}{2}$ lemon
pinch grated nutmeg
4 tbsp cream
4 oz long grain rice
3 hard-boiled eggs, finely chopped
2 teasp dried dill

salt and pepper
8 oz shortcrust pastry
1 egg yolk

Put the boiling fowl into a pan with
1 sliced onion, the celery, bay leaf,
peppercorns and water. Bring to the
boil and simmer for about $1\frac{1}{4}$ hours,
until the chicken is tender. Remove
the chicken from the pan and allow
to cool. Reserve the stock. Remove
all the meat from the chicken
carcass in small pieces. Melt half
the butter in a pan and add the
sliced mushrooms. Fry gently for a
few minutes. Mix with the chicken,
chopped parsley, lemon juice,
nutmeg, 3 tbsp of the cream and 4
tbsp of the stock. Season to taste.
Put the rice into a pan with $\frac{2}{3}$ pint of
the stock. Bring to the boil and
simmer for about 15 minutes, until
the rice is tender and the liquid
absorbed. Heat the rest of the butter
and fry the remaining sliced onion
gently until soft. Stir the fried
onions into the cooked rice. Mix the
chopped hard-boiled eggs with the
dill. Grease a rectangular ovenproof
dish. Spread a third of the rice
mixture into the dish. Cover with
half the chicken mixture, and then
half of the egg and dill. Repeat the
layers, finishing with a layer of rice.
Roll the pastry to make a rectangle
large enough to cover the dish.

Lay the pastry over the filling,
pressing the edges against the sides
of the dish. Trim off any excess
pastry. Make a hole in the centre
of the pastry to allow the steam to
escape. Mix the remaining tbsp
cream with the egg yolk and use to
glaze the pastry. Bake at 400°F,
Mark 6, for 15 minutes. Reduce the
heat to 350°F, Mark 4, and bake for
a further 30–40 minutes, until the
pastry crust is golden brown. Serve
warm.

(American: 6 tbsp butter, $1\frac{1}{4}$ cups
button mushrooms, 5 cups water,
$\frac{1}{2}$ cup rice)

Spain:
Paella

Serves 6
6 chicken thighs
1 onion, finely chopped
3 tbsp oil
12 oz long grain rice
2 pints chicken stock
$\frac{1}{2}$ teasp powdered saffron (alter-
    natively, use yellow colouring)
1 red pepper, chopped
salt and pepper
6 oz *chorizo* or similar sausage,
    chopped
$\frac{1}{2}$ pint prawns in their shells, washed
chopped parsley

Fry the chicken thighs and onion
gently in the oil until lightly golden.
Add the rice, stock and saffron and
bring to the boil. Add the red

pepper, seasoning, sausage and prawns and simmer for 20 minutes or until the rice is tender and the liquid absorbed. Serve very hot, sprinkled with chopped parsley.

(American: 5 cups stock, 1½ cups long grain rice, 1 cup prawns)

*Pollo chilindron

Serves 4
2 cloves garlic, crushed
6 tbsp oil
1 onion, chopped
1 lb tomatoes, skinned, seeded and
   chopped
2 large poussins, split in half
salt and pepper
½ lb lean ham, cut into strips
4 red peppers, chopped
2 tbsp chopped parsley

Fry the garlic and onion gently in half the oil. Add the tomatoes and simmer gently for 30 minutes, until pulpy. Brown the split chickens in the remaining oil. Add the seasoning, ham, red pepper and chopped parsley. Stir in the tomato sauce. Cover the pan and simmer gently for about 30 minutes, until the chicken is tender.

Italy:
Insalata di riso e pollo

Serves 4

This dish is usually served as an hors d'oeuvre, but it can make a delicious light main meal in summer. Prepare it at least 2 hours before needed, to allow the flavours to mingle.

6 oz long grain rice
salt and pepper
6 tbsp olive oil
2 tbsp wine vinegar
good pinch ground nutmeg
¾ lb cooked chicken, off the bone
4 oz button mushrooms, sliced
1 small head of fennel, finely
   shredded

Cook the long grain rice in boiling salted water until just tender. Drain. Stir in the olive oil, vinegar, nutmeg and seasoning while the rice is still warm. Pull the chicken into strips. Stir the chicken, mushrooms and fennel into the rice.

(American: ¾ cup rice, ⅔ cup mushrooms)

Greece:
*Kota kapama

Serves 4
2 oz butter
3 tbsp oil

8 small chicken joints
salt and pepper
1 onion, finely chopped
1 clove garlic, crushed
1 lb tomatoes, skinned, seeded
  and chopped
2 tbsp tomato puree
$\frac{1}{4}$ pint chicken stock
piece cinnamon stick (or $\frac{1}{4}$ teasp
  ground cinnamon)
grated Parmesan cheese (see below)

Heat the butter and oil in a large frying pan. Add the chicken to the pan, season to taste, and brown on all sides. Remove the chicken to a plate. Tip off most of the fat from the pan, leaving about 1 tbsp. Add the onion and garlic and cook until lightly golden. Add the tomatoes, tomato puree, stock, cinnamon and seasoning. Bring to the boil. Add the chicken to the sauce. Cover the pan and simmer gently for 30 minutes, until the chicken is tender. Arrange the chicken on a serving dish and spoon over the sauce. Serve with grated Parmesan cheese.

In Greece a Cephalonian cheese called *Kefalotiri* is used. This can be bought from some delicatessens and specialist food shops.

(American: 4 tbsp butter, $\frac{2}{3}$ cup chicken stock)

Turkey:
*Cerkes tavugu

Serves 6 as a first course
3 lb chicken
1 pint water
salt and pepper
4 oz walnut halves
1 onion, finely chopped
3 slices white bread, diced and the
  crusts removed
$\frac{1}{2}$ teasp paprika
2 tbsp chopped parsley

Put the chicken into a saucepan with the water and seasoning. Cover and simmer about 1 hour, until the chicken is just tender. Remove the chicken and allow to cool. Measure off $\frac{1}{2}$ pint stock. Put into the liquidizer with the walnuts and onion. Blend for 30 seconds. Add the bread, paprika and seasoning. Blend to give a smooth puree. (Alternatively, pound the dry ingredients together, mix with stock and sieve.) Remove the skin from the chicken and pull the flesh into strips. Put the chicken into a bowl and stir in half the walnut sauce. Arrange the chicken on a serving dish and spoon over the remaining walnut sauce. Sprinkle with chopped parsley.

(American: 2$\frac{1}{2}$ cups water, $\frac{2}{3}$ cup walnut halves)

Middle East: Dajaj mahshi

Serves 4
4 oz butter
1 onion, finely chopped
3½ lb chicken
2 oz pine kernels
6 oz long grain rice
¾ pint stock
2 oz currants
salt and pepper
¼ pint natural yogurt

Melt half the butter in a deep pan. Add the onion and fry gently until soft. Add the giblets from the chicken and the pine kernels and brown lightly. Add the rice and stir until the grains are glossy. Add the stock, currants and seasoning. Bring to the boil and simmer until the rice is tender and has absorbed the liquid. Stir in the remaining butter. Stuff the chicken with ⅓ of the rice mixture and truss to keep the chicken in good shape and enclose the stuffing. Put the chicken into a roasting dish. Mix the yogurt with seasoning and spread half the mixture over the chicken. Roast at 400°F, Mark 6, for 15 minutes. Spread with the remaining yogurt mixture. Reduce the oven heat to 350°F, Mark 4, and roast for a further hour, until the chicken is tender. Warm the remaining rice through in a saucepan and serve as an accompaniment to the roast chicken.

(American: ½ cup butter, ¾ cup long grain rice, 4 tbsp pine kernels, 1¼ cups stock, 4 tbsp currants, ⅔ cup yogurt)

India: Tandoori murg

Serves 4
3–3½ lb chicken
juice 2 lemons
1 tbsp salt
1 teasp powdered saffron
3 tbsp boiling water
1 teasp coriander seeds
1 teasp cumin seeds
small piece fresh ginger root, scraped and chopped (or 1 teasp ground ginger)
2 cloves garlic, crushed
½ pint natural yogurt
cochineal
½ teasp cayenne pepper
2 tbsp oil

Make several deep slits in the chicken with a sharp knife. Mix the lemon juice with the salt and rub well into the surface of the chicken. Put the chicken into a dish. Dissolve the saffron in the boiling water and pour over the chicken.

Toast the coriander and cumin seeds under the grill. Put them into a liquidizer with the ginger, garlic and yogurt and blend until smooth, or pound together with pestle and mortar. Stir in about $\frac{1}{2}$ teasp cochineal, to give a deep pink colour, and the cayenne pepper. This mixture is called *masala*. Spread the masala evenly over the chicken. Cover the dish with a lid or foil and refrigerate for 12 hours.

Stand the chicken on a rack in a roasting tin. Pour the oil and any liquid in the dish over the chicken. Roast at 400°F, Mark 6, for 15 minutes. Reduce the heat to 350°F, Mark 4, and cook for a further $1\frac{1}{4}$ hours. Cut chicken into serving pieces and serve with *salat* – a salad made from slivers of onion, sliced tomato, radishes, quarters of lemon, split chillies, lemon juice and salt and pepper.

(American: $1\frac{1}{4}$ cups natural yogurt)

Japan:
Yakitori

Serves 4
3 tbsp soy sauce
3 tbsp sake (rice wine)
2 teasp sugar
small piece fresh ginger root, sliced thinly
$\frac{1}{2}$ lb chicken livers
4 boned chicken breasts, cut into cubes

8 large spring onions, cut into chunks
$\frac{1}{2}$ pint teriyaki sauce (see below)
Japanese or ground black pepper

Mix the soy sauce, sake, sugar and ginger in a bowl. Add the whole chicken livers. Leave to marinate overnight in the refrigerator. Remove the livers from the marinade and cut in half. Thread the halved chicken livers onto 4 small skewers. Thread 8 larger skewers with the pieces of chicken alternated with spring onion. Dip the skewers into teriyaki sauce. Grill on one side for 4 minutes. Dip the skewers once again into the sauce and grill on the other side for 4 minutes. Serve one chicken liver and 2 chicken and spring onion skewers per person, with a little of the teriyaki sauce spooned over and sprinkled with pepper.

Teriyaki sauce can be bought from oriental food shops and most delicatessens.

(American: 1 cup chicken livers, $1\frac{1}{4}$ cups teriyaki sauce)

Puerto Rico:
Asopao

Serves 6
8 small chicken joints
1 clove garlic, crushed

2 teasp salt
1 teasp dried oregano
3 tbsp oil
1 onion, finely chopped
1 green pepper, finely chopped
2 oz lean ham, cut into small pieces
6 tomatoes, skinned, seeded and
   chopped
8 oz can tomatoes
12 oz long grain rice
$2\frac{1}{2}$ pints stock
salt and pepper
small packet frozen peas
2 oz grated Parmesan cheese
2 oz stuffed olives, sliced
1 tbsp capers

Skin the chicken joints. Mix the garlic, salt and oregano and rub well into the chicken. Heat the oil in a large pan and fry the chicken until golden brown. Remove the chicken to a plate. Fry the onion and pepper gently in the remaining fat.

Stir in the ham, tomatoes and canned tomatoes and simmer until the mixture forms a thick pulp. Add the chicken pieces. Cover and simmer for about 30 minutes, until the chicken is tender. Remove the chicken once again to a plate. Stir in the rice, stock and seasoning. Bring to the boil and simmer for 20 minutes, until the rice is tender. The mixture should be soupy in consistency: the Caribbean term is *asopao*. Stir in the peas, grated Parmesan, olives, capers and chicken. Cover and simmer for a few minutes, until the chicken is heated through. Serve at once, straight from the pan.

(American: 4 tbsp chopped ham, $\frac{2}{3}$ cup canned tomatoes, $1\frac{1}{2}$ cups rice, $6\frac{1}{4}$ cups stock, 4 tbsp Parmesan cheese, 4 tbsp stuffed olives)

Chicken miscellania: sauces, stuffings and butters

The trimmings and accompaniments can make or mar a chicken dish, and it is worth giving a little thought to which will best go with a particular dish.

As a general guide, an accompaniment with a sharp flavour such as Cider Barbecue Sauce (p 59) offsets richly cooked chicken well; whereas the blandness of boiled and poached chicken is complimented by a creamy, tasty sauce such as Creamy Avocado Sauce (p 57).

All the stuffings in this section can be used for a whole chicken or poussins, and of course for other poultry and game. Remember that if you are boning and stuffing a chicken you need a firm, compact stuffing rather than one that contains loose pieces of fruit and vegetable.

I give three ideas for flavoured butters in this section, but many others can be made up. In each case the soft butter is rolled into a sausage shape, put into greaseproof paper and chilled until quite firm. The chilled butter is cut into slices and served on top of hot grilled or shallow fried chicken or inside boned chicken breasts, as in the recipe for Pollo Sorpresa (see p 33).

Herbed bread sauce

Serves 4–6
$\frac{1}{4}$ pint milk
$\frac{1}{4}$ pint cream
bay leaf
few cloves
4 large slices wholemeal bread
2 oz butter
1 onion, finely chopped
salt and pepper
1 egg yolk

Put the milk and cream into a pan with the bay leaf, cloves and seasoning. Bring to the boil, remove from the heat, and add the crumbled slices of bread. Leave to stand for 30 minutes. Melt the butter and fry the onion gently until soft. Stir in the steeped bread mixture and the egg yolk. Stir over a gentle heat, until heated through. Adjust seasoning to taste.

(American: $\frac{2}{3}$ pint milk, $\frac{2}{3}$ pint cream, 4 tbsp butter)

*Cranberry sauce

Makes approximately $\frac{1}{2}$ pint
$\frac{1}{2}$ lb cranberries
$\frac{1}{4}$ pint orange juice
4 oz granulated sugar
juice $\frac{1}{2}$ lemon

Put the cranberries into a pan with the orange juice, sugar and lemon juice. Cover and simmer gently until the fruit is just tender. Serve cold.

(American: $1\frac{1}{2}$ cups cranberries, $\frac{2}{3}$ cup orange juice, $\frac{1}{2}$ cup sugar)

*Port wine sauce

Makes approximately 1 pint
1 small onion, finely chopped
2 tbsp butter
2 tbsp flour
grated rind and juice $\frac{1}{2}$ orange
pinch ground cinnamon
$\frac{1}{2}$ pint chicken stock
$\frac{1}{4}$ pint port
4 tbsp redcurrant jelly
salt and pepper

Fry the onion gently in the butter until soft. Stir in the flour and cook for 1 minute. Add the orange rind and juice, ground cinnamon, stock, port, redcurrant jelly and seasoning. Bring to the boil, stirring, and simmer until the sauce is thickened.

(American: $1\frac{1}{4}$ cups chicken stock, $\frac{2}{3}$ cup port)

Creamy avocado sauce

Makes 1 pint
$\frac{1}{2}$ pint chicken stock
$\frac{1}{4}$ pint double cream
1 egg yolk
1 large ripe avocado pear, peeled and chopped
salt and pepper
grated rind $\frac{1}{2}$ lemon
1 small onion, chopped

Put all the ingredients into the liquidizer and blend until smooth.

Alternatively, mix together and sieve. Put into a saucepan and heat through gently. Do not allow to boil.

(American: $1\frac{1}{4}$ cups chicken stock, $\frac{2}{3}$ cup heavy cream)

Lemon and almond sauce

Makes approximately 1 pint
4 oz blanched almonds
$\frac{1}{2}$ pint chicken stock
juice and grated rind 1 lemon
2 tbsp sugar
$\frac{1}{4}$ pint double cream
salt and pepper

Put the almonds into a pan with the stock, lemon juice, rind and sugar. Bring to the boil and simmer for 20 minutes. Blend in the liquidizer until smooth. Return to the saucepan and stir in the cream and seasoning to taste. Heat through gently, without boiling.

(American: $\frac{2}{3}$ cup blanched almonds, $1\frac{1}{4}$ cups chicken stock, $\frac{2}{3}$ cup heavy cream)

*Orange and raisin sauce

Makes approximately 1 pint
3 oz raisins
$\frac{1}{2}$ pint chicken stock
$\frac{1}{2}$ pint fresh orange juice
juice $\frac{1}{2}$ lemon
1 tbsp cornflour

Put the raisins into a saucepan with the stock. Bring just to the boil. Remove from the heat and leave the raisins in the hot stock for $\frac{1}{2}$ hour to plump. Add all the orange juice, apart from 2 tbsp, and the lemon juice to the pan. Bring back to the boil. Blend the cornflour with the remaining orange juice, and stir in the hot liquid gradually. Bring the sauce to the boil and stir until thickened. Serve hot.

(American: 6 tbsp raisins, $1\frac{1}{4}$ cups chicken stock, $1\frac{1}{4}$ cups fresh orange juice)

*Honeyed pineapple sauce

Makes approximately 1 pint
1 can crushed pineapple
    (approximately 10 fl oz)
4 tbsp clear honey
juice 1 lemon
1 tbsp cornflour
$\frac{1}{4}$ pint cream

Put the crushed pineapple into a pan with the honey and lemon juice. Stir over the heat to dissolve the honey. Blend the cornflour with a little water and stir into the pineapple mixture. Bring to the boil, stirring, until thickened. Stir in the cream and heat through gently.

(American: $1\frac{1}{4}$ cups crushed pineapple, $\frac{2}{3}$ cup cream)

*Cider barbecue sauce

Makes approximately 1 pint
2 onions, chopped
1 oz butter
1 tbsp French mustard
3 tbsp vinegar
2 tbsp tomato puree
8 oz can peeled tomatoes
½ pint cider
1 tbsp Worcester sauce
1 tbsp cornflour
salt and pepper

Fry the onions gently in the butter until soft. Add the French mustard, vinegar, tomato puree, canned tomatoes, cider and Worcester sauce. Bring to the boil and simmer for 10 minutes. Blend the cornflour with a little water and stir into the sauce. Stir over the heat until thickened. Season to taste. Can be served either hot or cold.

(American: 2 tbsp butter, 1 cup peeled tomatoes, 1¼ cups cider)

Mayonnaise

Makes ½ pint
2 egg yolks
1 tbsp wine vinegar
2 teasp French mustard
2 teasp caster sugar
½ pint olive oil
salt and pepper

Beat the egg yolks with the vinegar, then add the mustard and sugar.

Gradually whisk in the olive oil, in a fine trickle, until all the oil has been absorbed. Season to taste. If the mayonnaise is too thick, add a little hot water.

(American: 1¼ cups oil)

*Six herb stuffing

Sufficient for 3½ lb chicken
1 onion, chopped
2 oz butter
6 oz fresh white breadcrumbs
2 tbsp chopped parsley
½ tbsp chopped fresh marjoram
½ tbsp chopped fresh basil
½ tbsp chopped fresh thyme
½ tbsp chopped fresh oregano
½ tbsp chopped fresh tarragon
salt and pepper
2 eggs, beaten

Fry the onion gently in the butter. Mix with the white breadcrumbs, chopped herbs, seasoning and beaten egg.

Note: if using dried herbs, use only ½ teasp of each.

(American: 4 tbsp butter, 1½ cups breadcrumbs)

Vegetable stuffing

Sufficient for 3½ lb chicken
2 onions, sliced
4 stems celery, chopped
2 leeks, thinly sliced
2 oz butter

3 carrots, grated
$\frac{1}{4}$ lb button mushrooms, chopped
3 tbsp chopped parsley
1 teasp mixed herbs
1 clove garlic, crushed
salt and pepper
1 egg, beaten

Fry the onion, celery and leek gently in the butter. Add the grated carrot and mushrooms and fry for a further few minutes. Stir in the remaining ingredients.

Other vegetables can be used in place of those listed, for example grated potato, small florets of cauliflower, sliced courgettes.

*Bacon oatmeal stuffing

Sufficient for $3\frac{1}{2}$ lb chicken
4 rashers bacon, chopped
2 onions, sliced
2 oz butter
4 oz oatmeal
3 oz shredded suet
2 eggs, beaten
salt and pepper
4 tbsp chopped parsley

Fry the chopped bacon and onion gently in the butter until soft. Mix with the oatmeal, suet, beaten eggs, seasoning and parsley.

This is quite a sticky stuffing when made up, but it becomes firmer on cooking.

(American: 1 cup oatmeal, $\frac{3}{4}$ cup shredded suet)

Spinach and egg stuffing

Sufficient for $3\frac{1}{2}$ lb chicken
1 lb fresh spinach (or 1 large
    packet frozen spinach)
1 onion, chopped
2 oz butter
pinch grated nutmeg
salt and pepper
4 hard-boiled eggs, chopped
2 egg yolks
grated rind $\frac{1}{2}$ lemon

Cook the spinach in a little boiling salted water, until just tender. Drain thoroughly and chop. Fry the onion gently in the butter. Mix with the drained spinach and the remaining ingredients.

(American: 4 tbsp butter)

Cheese and nut stuffing

Sufficient for $3\frac{1}{2}$ lb chicken
2 onions, grated
6 oz fresh white breadcrumbs
2 oz melted butter
salt and pepper
3 oz toasted almonds, chopped
3 oz pkt rich full fat cheese
4 tbsp milk
1 egg, beaten
4 oz Edam cheese, cut into small
   cubes

Mix the grated onions with the breadcrumbs, melted butter, seasoning and chopped nuts. Soften the cream cheese and beat together with the milk. Add the milk and cheese mixture to the stuffing, together with the beaten egg and cubes of cheese.

(American: 1½ cups breadcrumbs, 4 tbsp melted butter, ½ cup toasted almonds, ⅓ cup cream cheese, ⅔ cup cubed Edam cheese)

*Prune, apple and walnut stuffing

Sufficient for 3½ lb chicken
4 oz dried prunes
½ pint red wine
piece cinnamon stick
grated rind 1 lemon
6 slices wholemeal bread
3 oz chopped walnuts (or other
    nuts if preferred)
2 dessert apples, cored and sliced
2 oz butter

Soak the prunes in the red wine for 6 hours, or overnight. Drain the prunes, remove the stones and chop. Put the prune liquid into a pan with the cinnamon stick and lemon rind. Bring to the boil. Remove from the heat and add the wholemeal bread, broken into pieces. Leave to become quite cold, until the bread has absorbed all the liquid. Remove the cinnamon stick and add the chopped prunes and walnuts. Fry the apple slices gently in the butter until lightly golden. Add to the remaining stuffing ingredients.

(American: 1 cup dried prunes,

1¼ cups red wine, ½ cup walnuts, 4 tbsp butter)

*Sweet bread stuffing

Sufficient for 3½ lb chicken
1 onion, finely chopped
2 oz butter
½ lb malt bread, crumbled
2 eating apples, grated
grated rind ½ lemon
little cream to mix

Fry the onion gently in the butter. Add the malt bread and the grated apple. Stir in the lemon rind and sufficient cream to give a firm but moist stuffing. This should be quite a sweet stuffing, but seasoning can be added if liked.

(American: 4 tbsp butter)

*Chestnut and apricot stuffing

Sufficient for 3½ lb chicken
4 oz dried apricots
1 onion, chopped
2 oz butter
15 oz can unsweetened chestnut
    puree
grated rind ½ orange
salt and pepper
3 oz fresh breadcrumbs
1 egg, beaten

Soak the apricots in sufficient boiling water to just cover for 6 hours, or overnight. Drain the apricots, reserving the liquid, and chop. Fry the onion gently in the butter for a few minutes. Mix with

the chestnut puree, chopped
apricots, orange rind, seasoning
and breadcrumbs. Add sufficient of
the apricot liquid to give a soft but
firm consistency.

Banana and date stuffing

Sufficient for 3½ lb chicken

*Fresh dates are the best for this
recipe, but if they are difficult to
obtain dried ones can be used instead.*

1 onion, chopped
2 oz butter
grated rind and juice ½ lemon
6 oz fresh breadcrumbs
1 egg, beaten
4 tbsp soured cream
salt and pepper
2 bananas, chopped
4 oz fresh dates, stoned and chopped

First toast the breadcrumbs: oil a
baking sheet generously, and
scatter the breadcrumbs evenly over
the surface. Cook in a moderate
oven until golden. Stir breadcrumbs
and return to the oven for a further
few minutes. Fry the onion gently in
the butter until soft. Mix with the
remaining ingredients.

(American: 4 tbsp butter, 1½ cups
breadcrumbs, 1 cup chopped dates)

*Citrus stuffing

Sufficient for 3½ lb chicken
6 thick slices bread, cut into
    small cubes

oil for deep frying
2 oz melted butter
grated rind 1 lemon
grated rind 1 orange
segments from 1 grapefruit,
    chopped
2 oz brown sugar
1 onion, grated
salt and pepper

Deep fry the cubes of bread in hot
oil until crisp and golden. Drain on
absorbent paper. Mix the fried
bread cubes with the remaining
ingredients.

(American: 4 tbsp melted butter,
4 tbsp brown sugar)

*Tarragon and lemon butter

4 oz softened butter
grated rind and juice ½ lemon
1 tbsp chopped fresh tarragon
salt and pepper

Beat the softened butter with the
lemon rind, juice, tarragon and
seasoning to taste.

(American: ½ cup butter)

*Curried parsley butter

4 oz softened butter
2 teasp curry powder
3 tbsp chopped parsley

Beat the softened butter with the
curry powder and chopped parsley.
No extra seasoning is necessary.

(American: ½ cup butter)

*Devilled butter

4 oz softened butter
2 teasp French mustard
2 teasp Worcester sauce
2 teasp tomato puree
salt and pepper

Beat the softened butter with the French mustard, Worcester sauce, tomato puree and seasoning to taste.

Index

Chicken
 carving 8
 choosing and buying 5
 cooking 8
 freezing 6
 storing 6
 trussing 7

Chicken for cold dishes
 introduction 40
 Chicken and bean
  sprout salad 43
 Chicken with blue cheese
  and bacon sauce 44
 Chicken with
  guacamole 43
 Chicken and lettuce
  dolmas 42
 Chicken Peter Heering 44
 Chicken ratatouille
  salad 43
 Chicken with peanut
  sauce 44
 Chicken terrine 41
 Chicken veronique 45
 Chilled chicken curry 41
 Hawaiian chicken salad 42
 Jellied chicken with
  champagne 46
 Spiced chicken in milk 45

Chicken for the frying pan
 introduction 29
 Chicken and bacon
  croquettes 31
 Chicken in basket 30
 Chicken maryland 32
 Chicken with orange and
  sherry sauce 33

Chinese style stir fried
 chicken 32
Creamy chicken with
 chestnuts 30
Pollo sorpresa 33
Quick chicken creole 30
Spatchcock chicken 31

Chicken for the grill
 introduction 35
 Barbecued apricot
  chicken 38
 Cheesy grilled chicken 38
 Chicken avocado grills 39
 Chicken kebabs 36
 Chicken limey 37
 Chicken and mushroom
  rarebits 39
 Garlic and cream
  chicken 36
 Simple barbecued
  drumsticks 38
 Simple curried chicken 36
 Skewered drumsticks 38

Chicken miscellania
 introduction 56
 Bacon and oatmeal
  stuffing 60
 Banana and date
  stuffing 62
 Cheese and nut stuffing 60
 Chestnut and apricot
  stuffing 61
 Cider barbecue sauce 59
 Citrus stuffing 62
 Cranberry sauce 57
 Creamy avocado sauce 57
 Curried parsley butter 62

Devilled butter 63
Herbed bread sauce 57
Honeyed pineapple
 sauce 58
Lemon and almond
 sauce 58
Mayonnaise 59
Orange and raisin sauce 58
Port wine sauce 57
Prune, apple and walnut
 stuffing 61
Six herb stuffing 59
Spinach and egg stuffing 60
Sweet bread stuffing 61
Tarragon and lemon
 butter 62
Vegetable stuffing 59

Chicken for the oven
 introduction 18
 Baked chicken with
  ratatouille 22
 Chicken and leek pie 23
 Chicken with mixed fruit
  stuffing 19
 Chicken saltimbocca 21
 Corn bread chicken 20
 Moussaka chicken 22
 Normandy chicken 21
 Orange glazed chicken 19
 Savoury chicken
  roulade 20
 Spiced lemon chicken 19
 Tasty bake chicken 21

Chicken for the pot
 introduction 24
 Chicken and beer
  casserole 25

Chicken
  bourguignonne 27
Chicken and cabbage
  hotpot 26
Chicken paprika 25
Chicken and vegetable
  casserole 26
Coq au vin 28
Normandy chicken
  casserole 26
Pickled chicken 27
Sweet sour chicken 25

Chicken for starters
  introduction 12
Avocado and chicken
  soup 13
Chicken avocado
  vinaigrette 14

Chicken and cheese pie 14
Chicken and cream cheese
  mousse 14
Chicken and cucumber
  soup 13
Chicken nicoise 15
Chicken skordalia 15
Chicken and sweetcorn
  quiches 16
Chicken and tomato
  soup 13
Chilled spiced chicken 16
Curried chicken and
  prawns 15
Devilled chicken
  croutes 17

Foreign ways with chicken
  introduction 47

Asopao (Puerto Rico) 55
Cerkes tavugu (Turkey) 52
Dajaj mahshi (Middle
  East) 53
Fricassee de Poulet
  (France) 48
Insalata di riso e pollo
  (Italy) 51
Kota kapama (Greece) 51
Kurnik (Russia) 49
Paella (Spain) 50
Pollo chilindron (Spain) 51
Poulet saute vallee
  d'Auge (France) 48
Stegt kylling
  (Denmark) 49
Tandoori murg (India) 53
Yakitori (Japan) 54
Weights and measures 11